contents

About the Editors   vii

About the Contributors   ix

Introduction   xvii

SECTION 1

PERSONALIZING↔POLITICIZING GENDER/ED REALITIES

1. **"Amnistia y legalizacion": Gendered Immigration in the Heartland,** by Victoria Pruin DeFrancisco and Karen Mitchell   **3**

2. **"What Do You Mean 'Just a Girl?'": Sergeant Stiles and a Media-Military Crisis,** by John W. Howard III and Laura C. Prividera   **9**

3. **"Being Homeless and Gay or Lesbian Is a Difficult Combination": An Invisible Population,** by Renee Houston   **16**

4. **To Guard or Not Guard?: Dilemmas Surrounding the Human Papillomavirus Vaccine,** by Marie Thompson and Lynn M. Harter   **19**

5. **"Heaping Hostility on Hillary": "Isms" in the 2008 Presidential Race,** by Lynn H. Turner and Patricia A. Sullivan   **25**

SECTION 2

(RE)ACTING GENDER/ED REALITIES

6. **"Pressure to Perform": The Challenges and Limitations of a Masculine Identity,** by M. Chad McBride   **35**

7. **"Only Skinny Girls Get the Roles": Body Image in the Dance World,** by Paige P. Edley   **42**

8. **"What Are We Supposed to Do, Mom?": A Lesson in Gender from a Bird in the Fireplace,** by Deborah S. Ballard-Reisch and Alyssa C. Ballard-Reisch   **45**

9. **"If It Makes You Uncomfortable, Get Over It": Sex Talk in the Physician-Patient Relationship,** by Jay Baglia   **47**

⑩ **"Is It Because I'm Female?": Challenges to Young Female Instructors in the College Classroom,** by Karla Mason Bergen   53

⑪ **"Would You Ever Make a Guy Wear Eyeliner?": External Pressures to "Do" Gender,** by M. Chad McBride   55

SECTION 3

(RE)CREATING GENDER/ED REALITIES

⑫ **"Why Are There So Many Girls"?: Talking Gender and Adoption in a Lesbian Family,** by Elizabeth A. Suter   61

⑬ **"When Do I Get a Break?": Unexpected Emotions for a Stay-at-Home Dad,** by Caryn E. Medved   67

⑭ **"Do We Need to Make It Look Good?": Form, Function, and Femininity for Women with Disabilities,** by Laura L. Ellingson   69

⑮ **"It Can't Be Domestic Violence . . . We're Just Dating": Keia's Story,** by Loreen N. Olson and Sacheen K. Mobley   71

⑯ **"Can a Man Be a Feminist?": Moving from Dominance to Alliance,** by M. Chad McBride   78

⑰ **"Starting Life with a Clean Slate": Kylie's New Job,** by Sherianne Shuler   80

SECTION 4

(RE)EVALUATING GENDER/ED REALITIES

⑱ **Dan's Question: Can Two Gay White Men Successfully Parent a Three-Year-Old African American Girl?,** by Kathleen M. Galvin and Dennis Patrick   85

⑲ **Money *or* Family/Money *for* Family: Fatherhood Dilemmas for Men of Differing Socioeconomic Classes,** by Suzy D'Enbeau, Patrice Buzzanell and John Duckworth   92

⑳ **"You Don't Just *Not* Get Married": The Normalization of Gender Role Expectations,** by Karen L. Daas   99

㉑ **"This Just Isn't Working Out": Gender, Technology, and Work/Family,** by Annis G. Golden   105

㉒ **Undercover Moms, Family CEOs, and "Opt-Out Revolution" Moms: Work-Life Possibilities for Women,** by Erika L. Kirby and M. Chad McBride   108

GENDER ACTUALIZED

CASES IN COMMUNICATIVELY CONSTRUCTING REALITIES

ERIKA L. KIRBY

M. CHAD MCBRIDE

Creighton University

KENDALL/HUNT PUBLISHING COMPANY
4050 Westmark Drive   Dubuque, Iowa 52002

Book Team

Chairman and Chief Executive Officer *Mark C. Falb*
President and Chief Operating Office *Chad M. Chandlee*
Vice President, Higher Education *David L. Tart*
Director of National Book Program *Paul B. Carty*
Editorial Development Manager *Georgia Botsford*
Senior Developmental Editor *Angela Willenbring*
Assistant Vice President, Production Services *Christine E. O'Brien*
Senior Production Editor *Carrie Maro*
Permissions Editor *Colleen Zelinsky*
Cover Designer *Janell Edwards*

Copyright © 2009 by Kendall/Hunt Publishing Company

ISBN 978-0-7575-5988-4
Special Edition ISBN 978-0-7575-6041-5

Printed in the United States of America
10 9 8 7 6 5 4 3 2 1

㉓ **"I Feel Like I Won't Be a Good Mom if I Don't at Least *Try*":**
The Breastfeeding Debate, by Sherianne Shuler   **115**

SECTION 5

REPRODUCING↔CHALLENGING GENDER/ED REALITIES

㉔ **"How Is *That* Going to Work?": Explaining Commuter Marriage**
to Others, by Karla Mason Bergen   **123**

㉕ **"Look, Not Everybody Can Get Pregnant!": When Private Issues**
Are Made Public, by Jennifer J. Bute   **130**

㉖ **"You're Totally Her Work Husband": Managing Misconceptions in the**
"Work-Spouse" Relationship, by M. Chad McBride and Erika L. Kirby   **133**

㉗ **"With You We Got a Twofer": Challenging the Affirmative Action Hire**
Stereotype, by Brenda J. Allen   **139**

㉘ **"Don't Be So Gay!": Challenging Homophobic Language,** by Erika L. Kirby   **141**

SECTION 6

(RE)POSITIONING GENDER/ED REALITIES

㉙ **"I Never Hit Her": Abuse between Intimates,** by Julia T. Wood   **147**

㉚ **"Like the Marines, Do We Need a Few Good Men?": Contesting the**
Single-Sex Mandate of the YWCA, by Lynn M. Harter, Erika L. Kirby,
and Margaret M. Quinlan   **153**

㉛ **"Our ~~Father~~ Creator Who Art in Heaven . . .": Negotiating Patriarchy**
in Religion and Feminism, by Erika L. Kirby   **159**

㉜ **"If a Boy Is Playing with It, It's a Boy Toy; If a Girl Is Playing with It,**
It's a Girl Toy": Questioning the Gendering of Toys, by Paaige K. Turner   **162**

㉝ **"Let Me Work the Kinks Out of Your Neck": The Story of Jared and**
Chris, by Diana K. Ivy and Shawn T. Wahl   **164**

㉞ **Making Ourselves a(t) Home in Academia: The "Creatively Welcoming"**
Space of OSCLG, by Cynthia Berryman-Fink, Cheris Kramarae, Bobby Patton,
Anita Taylor, and Virginia E. Wheeless   **170**

Index   **179**

about the editors

Erika L. Kirby (Ph.D., University of Nebraska-Lincoln) is a Professor and Chair of Communication Studies at Creighton University, where she has been since 1998. She studies organizational and applied communication and discourses, as well as their intersections with gender and feminism. Broadly speaking, she is interested in the everyday intersections of working and personal life, and has published widely in that area. Erika teaches various courses related to organizational communication as well as gender and a capstone entitled *Communication and Community.* Her research has appeared in the *Journal of Applied Communication Research, Management Communication Quarterly, Communication Monographs, Communication Yearbook,* the *Electronic Journal of Communication,* and the *Sage Handbook of Conflict Communication.* Her professional service has included serving as President and Conference Planner of the *Organization for the Study of Communication, Language, and Gender* (OSCLG), Chair of the Applied Communication Division of the National Communication Association, and reviewing for numerous journals. She has trained and consulted for multiple constituencies within Creighton University as well as in organizations outside of academe. She currently lives in Omaha, Nebraska with her partner Bob, daughters Meredith and Samantha, and cat Otis, but is originally from north central Iowa. Erika's education reflects these Midwestern roots—she received her B.A. from Buena Vista University in Storm Lake, Iowa and her M.A. from the University of Minnesota. Outside of her working life as a professor, Erika enjoys her daily "booty shaking" as a Jazzercise instructor.

M. Chad McBride (Ph.D., University of Nebraska-Lincoln) is an Assistant Professor of Communication Studies at Creighton University, where he has been since 2003. He studies communication and identity management within personal relationships and social networks (including families). He is interested in how individuals communicatively co-construct situated identities both in their social networks and in the larger culture as well as mediated communication about relationships. Chad teaches courses in interpersonal, family, small group, and gender communication, and the dreaded research methods course. His research has appeared in the *Journal of Social and Personal Relationships, Journal of Family Communication, Communication Studies, Communication Reports,* the *Electronic Journal of Communication,* and the *Sage Handbook of Conflict Communication.* His professional service has included serving as a Conference Planner and a Board Member of the *Organization for the Study of Communication, Language, and Gender* (OSCLG) and reviewing for numerous journals. Even though he currently enjoys living in Omaha, Nebraska, he is a born and bred Texan, and his family (including parents, siblings, niece, and nephews) is located in the Fort Worth area. He attended Texas Christian University for his B.A. and M.A. and is an avid Horned Frogs fan. Like many Texans, you will find him in his jersey cheering for the Dallas Cowboys on most Sundays in the fall. An avid music fan, Chad enjoys attending concerts of all genres and his MP3 player is part of his daily uniform.

about the contributors

Brenda J. Allen (Ph.D., Howard University) is an Associate Dean in the College of Liberal Arts and Sciences and a Professor in the Department of Communication at the University of Colorado Denver. Her research and teaching interests include organizational communication, social identity, and power dynamics. Her research has been published in numerous communication journals, and she is the author of a groundbreaking book entitled *Difference Matters: Communicating Social Identity.*

Jay Baglia (Ph.D., University of South Florida) is a Medical Educator at the Lehigh Valley Hospital and Health Network in Allentown, Pennsylvania. He is the author of the book *The Viagra Ad Venture: Masculinity, Media and the Performance of Sexual Health* and a Board Member of the Organization for the Study of Communication, Language and Gender (OSCLG).

Deborah S. Ballard-Reisch (Ph.D., Bowling Green State University) is the Kansas Health Foundation Distinguished Chair in Strategic Communication and Professor at the Elliott School of Communication at Wichita State University. She teaches and researches strategic communication, particularly as it relates to community-based participatory research, gender, personal relationships, family, culture, and health. Her research has appeared in numerous journals related to personal relationships, family(s), and health. Deborah enjoys world travel, hiking, and hanging out with her children, Stefan and Alyssa.

Alyssa C. Ballard-Reisch (Sophomore, Andover Central High School, Andover, Kansas) studies theater and dance and enjoys performing. She has been researching the way students interact with teachers based on gender and mother/daughter communication for almost five years. She has presented her work at the Organization for the Study of Communication, Language and Gender (OSCLG) Conferences. Alyssa enjoys hip-hop dancing, movies, hanging with friends, and playing with her dogs, Merlin and Jami.

Karla Mason Bergen (Ph.D., University of Nebraska-Lincoln) is Assistant Professor of Communication and Coordinator of Women's Studies at the College of Saint Mary in Omaha, Nebraska. Her research is focused on family communication and the social construction of identity, specifically how women communicatively negotiate unconventional identities. She has studied identity construction of female professors, lesbian families, and most recently, women in commuter marriages, and has published several articles and book chapters based on her research.

Cynthia Berryman-Fink (Ph.D., Bowling Green State University) is a Professor of Communication at the University of Cincinnati. She was co-convener of the first Organization for the Study of Communication, Language and Gender (OSCLG) conference in 1978 and co-editor of its first conference proceedings: *Communication, Language and Sex.* She has taught courses in gender communication and organizational diversity, published numerous books and articles on issues of gender and diversity, and served as a gender and diversity consultant to dozens of organizations.

Jennifer J. Bute (Ph.D., University of Illinois at Urbana-Champaign) is an Assistant Professor in the School of Communication Studies at Ohio University. She studies communication about health in interpersonal relationships and is particularly interested in issues related to privacy, social support, and gender. She teaches courses in health, interpersonal, and gender communication. Her work has appeared in *Health Communication, Human Communication Research, Qualitative Health Research,* and *Social Science and Medicine.*

Patrice M. Buzzanell (Ph.D., Purdue University) is Professor and the W. Charles and Ann Redding Faculty Fellow in the Department of Communication at Purdue University. Her teaching and research interests include careers, gender, leadership, and work-life issues. Her research has appeared in journals such as *Human Communication Research, Communication Monographs, Journal of Applied Communication Research, Human Relations, Management Communication Quarterly,* and *Journal of Family Communication.* She teaches in the Engineering Projects for Community Service.

Karen L. Daas (Ph.D., University of Nebraska-Lincoln) is an Assistant Professor of Communication at The University of Texas at San Antonio. She studies how women construct and negotiate personal and relational identities through communication and teaches courses in relational, gender, and small group communication. Her research has appeared in *Journal of Personal and Social Relationships, Journal of Family Communication, Journal of Family Issues,* and *Western Journal of Communication.*

Victoria Pruin DeFrancisco (Ph.D., University of Illinois, Champaign/Urbana) is a Professor of Communication Studies and Women's Studies at the University of Northern Iowa. Her areas of teaching and research interest are gender, language, and intercultural communication. One of her most recent publications is a textbook with Catherine Helen Palczewski, *Communicating Gender Diversity: A Critical Approach.*

Suzy D'Enbeau (M.A., Duquesne University) is a doctoral candidate in the Department of Communication at Purdue University. Her teaching and research interests include feminisms, consumerism, political economies, and work-life issues.

John D. Duckworth (M.A., Purdue University) is a financial planner in Chicago. His thesis, *The Discourse and Practice of Fatherhood: Identity Negotiations of Masculinities, Caregiving, and Work-Family Issues,* was the winner of the 2007 Outstanding Thesis Award from the Organization for the Study of Communication, Language and Gender (OSCLG).

Paige P. Edley (Ph.D., Rutgers University) is an Associate Professor at Loyola Marymount University. Her teaching and research interests include gender and power issues in organizational life, technology, and work-life balance, media influence on women's and girls' body image, communication advocacy and activism, ethics and corporate social responsibility, and women-owned businesses. Her research has appeared in *Management Communication Quarterly, Communication Yearbook, Women and Language, Electronic Journal of Communication,* and various books on communication, organizations, and gender issues.

Laura L. Ellingson (Ph.D., University of South Florida) is an Associate Professor of Communication at Santa Clara University. Her research focuses on gender, qualitative methodology, and interdisciplinary teamwork in health-care organizations. She is author of *Communicating in the Clinic: Negotiating Frontstage and Backstage Teamwork* and *Engaging Crystallization in Qualitative Research.* Currently she is conducting an ethnography of a dialysis clinic and collaborating with Dr. Patty Sotirin on a study of aunts' relationships with nieces and nephews.

Kathleen M. Galvin (Ph.D., Northwestern University) is a Professor of Communication Studies at Northwestern University. She studies discourse-dependent families, those that rely on communication to manage their familial identities, and family communication about health issues including genetic disease, fertility threatening cancer, and childhood cancer. Her courses include: family communication, relational communication, and communication theory. She is an author of eight books and the senior author of *Family Communication: Cohesion and Change* (7th ed.), and has published in the *Journal of Family Communication* and *Communication Yearbook.*

Annis G. Golden (Ph.D., Rensselaer Polytechnic Institute) is an Assistant Professor in the Department of Communication at the University at Albany, State University of New York. Her research focuses on women's and men's communicative management of their relationships to the organizations that employ them, including the ways these relationships are mediated by new information and communication technologies. She also studies women's health issues. Her work has appeared in *Human Relations, Management Communication Quarterly, Communication Yearbook, Journal of Family Communication,* and *Southern Communication Journal.*

Lynn M. Harter (Ph.D., University of Nebraska-Lincoln) is an Associate Professor and the Steven and Barbara Schoonover Professor of Health Communication in the School of Communication Studies at Ohio University and Senior Editor of *Health Communication.* Her scholarship focuses on the discourses of health and healing and organizing processes, feminist and narrative theory-praxis. She has published over 45 journal articles and book chapters, several books and edited volumes. She lives in Athens, Ohio, with her husband, Scott, daughter, Emma Grace, and hamster, Clara Belle.

Renee Houston (Ph.D., Florida State University) is an Associate Professor of Communication Studies at the University of Puget Sound. She studies organizational communication and her most recent research examines the intersections of public and organizational policy on women, the working poor, and the homeless. Her published research includes an edited volume, book chapters and journal articles that have appeared in *Communication Theory, Management Communication Quarterly,* and *International Journal of Learning.* She lives in Tacoma, Washington with her partner Eric and children Joshua and Julia.

John W. Howard, III (Ph.D., Bowling Green State University) is an Assistant Professor at East Carolina University. His main research interests are language and social interaction, aviation communication, nationalism, militarism, and gender and war. His work has been published in *Women and Language* and *Women's Studies in Communication,* and he has forthcoming pieces in *Human Communication Research* and the *International and Intercultural Communication Annual.*

Diana K. Ivy (Ph.D., University of Oklahoma) is Professor of Communication at Texas A&M University-Corpus Christi. She has been teaching college-level communication for 25 years, including such courses as nonverbal, interpersonal, gender, and instructional communication. She has co-authored three textbooks, two of which are in multiple editions, and has published articles in *Communication Education, Southern Communication Journal,* and *Women and Language.* She was awarded Outstanding Gender Scholar of the Year in 2002 by the Southern States Communication Association and serves as Archivist for the Women's Caucus of National Communication Association.

Cheris Kramarae (Ph.D., University of Illinois at Urbana-Champaign) is a Senior Research Associate, Center for the Study of Women in Society, at the University of Oregon. She taught one of the first language/gender courses in the United States and has served as a director of women's studies. Her research areas include gender and technology, education, and communication. She and Dale Spender are the editors of the four-volume *Routledge International Encyclopedia of Women: Global Women's Issues and Knowledge.*

Caryn E. Medved (Ph.D., University of Kansas) is an Associate Professor at Baruch College with the City University of New York. Her teaching and research interests form at the intersections between organizational and family communication, particularly related to identity, difference, and power. She is the current editor of *Journal of Family Communication.* Her work has appeared in *Management Communication Quarterly, Journal of Family Communication, Communication Yearbook, Journal of Applied Communication,* and *Journal of Marriage and Family.* She lives in New York City with her husband, Joe and their chocolate lab, Howard.

Karen Mitchell (Ph.D., Louisiana State University) is a Professor of Communication Studies at the University of Northern Iowa, where she teaches courses in performance studies and critical communication pedagogy. She is the Artistic Director of UNI Interpreters Theatre, and the founding director of SAVE (Students Against a Violent Environment) Forum Actors, and a former president of the organization Pedagogy and Theatre of the Oppressed.

Sacheen K. Mobley (M.A., University of Missouri-Kansas City) is a doctoral candidate in the Department of Communication at the University of Missouri-Columbia. She is an Interpersonal and Cultural Communication scholar whose research interests focus on questions of narrative and identity. Specifically, she studies master narratives and their influence on identity construction. She is currently working on her dissertation, looking at a theory of narrative identity.

Loreen N. Olson (Ph.D., University of Nebraska-Lincoln) is an Associate Professor of Communication at the University of Missouri-Columbia. Her teaching and research interests include interpersonal, family, and gender communication as well as the dark side of relationships and families and the social construction of identity. Her research has appeared in *Human Communication Research, Communication Theory, Communication Monographs,* and *Women's Studies in Communication.* Loreen lives in Columbia with husband Mark, twins Kenyon and Keaton, stepdaughters Aubrey and Julia, and toy poodles Freud and Einstein.

Dennis Patrick (Ph.D., The University of Texas-Austin) is a Professor of Communication at Eastern Michigan University. His research interests focus on family communication, especially as it relates to gay parenting and foster/adoptive families. He teaches courses in interpersonal, family, and gender communication. His most recent research appeared in *Child Welfare.* Dennis lives in Ypsilanti, Michigan with his partner Tom and sons Liam, Joshua, Paul, Joey, and Raul.

Bobby R. Patton (Ph.D., The University of Kansas) retired as President of the University of Central Missouri in 2005 after a 48-year-teaching career in communication studies. He was instrumental in the founding of the Organization for the Study of Communication, Language and Gender (OSCLG) and served three terms as president.

Laura C. Prividera (Ph.D., Bowling Green State University) is an Assistant Professor at East Carolina University. Her research interests include critical and feminist analyses of gender and race in instructional, military, health, and mediated contexts. Her work has been published in *Women and Language, Health Communication, Women's Studies in Communication,* and the *Basic Communication Course Annual.*

Margaret M. Quinlan (M.A., Illinois State University) is a doctoral candidate in the School of Communication Studies at Ohio University whose scholarly interests lie in the intersections between health and organizational communication. Her work focuses on a range of social-justice issues, including disability rights and gender inequities. She has published articles in *Text and Performance Quarterly, Communication Research Reports,* and *Health Communication.*

Sherianne Shuler (Ph.D., University of Kansas) is Associate Professor of Communication Studies at Creighton University. Her teaching and research focus on the public and private intersections of work, emotion, gender, and media. Her research has appeared in *American Communication Journal, Management Communication Quarterly, Women's Studies in Communication, The Electronic Journal of Communication, Communication Studies,* and in several edited volumes. She lives in Omaha, Nebraska with her partner, Nathan, and their spunky two-year-old, Lucy.

Patricia A. Sullivan (Ph.D., University of Iowa) is Professor of Communication and Chair of the Department of Communication and Media at the State University of New York, New Paltz. She specializes in the study of Rhetoric. Her current research projects focus on gender, race, and class issues in political communication, political apologies, and ethics and political communication. Her articles have appeared in *The Quarterly Journal of Speech, Western Journal of Communication, Communication Quarterly,* and *Women and Politics.*

Elizabeth A. Suter (Ph.D., University of Illinois at Urbana-Champaign) is an Assistant Professor of Human Communication Studies and is on the Gender and Women's Studies Faculty at the University of Denver. Her research takes a qualitative approach to the study of family, relational, and gender communication, with a particular focus on the discursive and symbolic negotiation of identities. Her work appears in *Sex Roles, Women and Language, Journal of Family Communication,* and the *Journal of Social and Personal Relationships.* She lives in Denver with her spouse and daughter.

Anita Taylor (Ph.D., University of Missouri-Columbia) is Professor Emerita of Communication and Women's Studies at George Mason University in Fairfax, Virginia. She has focused her scholarship in gender in communication for more than 20 years. She has edited the research periodical *Women and Language* since 1989. A vita is available at *http://comm.gmu.edu/faculty.*

Marie Thompson (M.A., Ohio University) is a doctoral student in the School of Communication Studies at Ohio University. Her scholarship focuses the gendered nature of health and healing and feminist perspectives on organizing.

Lynn H. Turner (Ph.D., Northwestern University) is Professor of Communication Studies and Interim Dean of the Diederich College of Communication at Marquette University. Her research areas include interpersonal, gendered, and family communication. Her articles have appeared in numerous journals and she has authored five books, including *Introducing Communication Theory, Perspectives on Family Communication,* and *The Family Communication Sourcebook,* all of which were co-authored/edited with Richard West. She is the current Second Vice President of the National Communication Association.

Paaige K. Turner (Ph.D., Purdue University) is an Associate Professor and Director of Graduate Studies at Saint Louis University. Her research looks at the creation and negotiation of contradiction, specifically the topics of organizational socialization, midwifery and birth, and the body in the workplace. Her work has appeared in *Midwifery Today, Management Communication Quarterly, Communication Monographs, Argumentation and Advocacy, Women and Language, Qualitative Health Research,* and *Qualitative Inquiry.*

Shawn T. Wahl (Ph.D., University of Nebraska-Lincoln) is an Associate Professor of Communication and Director of Graduate Studies at Texas A&M University-Corpus Christi. His research focuses on instructional communication and Internet studies and has appeared in *Communication Education, Journal of Family Communication, Communication Teacher, Review of Communication,* and *Basic Communication Course Annual.* Shawn is co-author of *The Nonverbal Self: Communication for a Lifetime* and *Business and Professional Excellence: KEYS to Communication in the Workplace.*

Virginia Eman Wheeless (Ph.D., University of Nebraska-Lincoln) is Professor of Communication at Texas A&M University-Corpus Christi. She was co-convener of the first Organization for the Study of Communication, Language and Gender (OSCLG) conference in 1978 and co-editor of its first conference proceedings: *Communication, Language, and Sex.* She has taught courses in interpersonal, organizational, and instructional communication, persuasion, and gender and communication. She has published numerous articles and book chapters on issues of gender and communication.

Julia T. Wood (Ph.D., Pennsylvania State University) is the Lineberger Distinguished Professor of Humanities and Professor of Communication Studies at the University of North Carolina at Chapel Hill. Her research and teaching focus on gender, intimate partner violence, and feminist theories, particularly feminist standpoint theory. During her career, she has published 23 books and more than 80 articles and chapters in books.

introduction

It was 2:30 P.M. when Erika suddenly realized she had not asked her students to do any outside applications for the unit on patriarchy they would be covering that day in her 3:00 P.M. gender course. She hurried into Chad's office, since he also taught the course. "Hey . . . I totally spaced out having the students apply patriarchy before coming to class today, and it can be a hard one for them to grasp. Got any ideas for what I can do in class now?"

"I can check my files," Chad said. As he ruffled through the cabinet he was inspired. "Do you know what would be really helpful in these situations? If there was some sort of collection of cases or stories that we could use to bring complex ideas like patriarchy to life."

"I would sure use a book like that, I have found that class time is most productive and students learn more when they connect with the course material on a personal level. With some of the more complex terms surrounding gender, it is particularly difficult to make that happen, so anything to help get us to application would really be productive."

When Erika arrived at school the next day, Chad walked into her office and announced: "Hey, I've got a crazy idea. You know how we were talking yesterday about how handy a collection of narratives would be for gender courses? I was thinking about it last night and it hit me: 'Why don't we write one?' "

The preceding narrative (which is loosely based on our reality) provides you with a preview of the style of this book wherein contributors have created narratives/cases to provide a common frame for dialoguing about gender/ed issues—a common frame for "actualizing" gender. Like the brief example of Erika and Chad, the cases you will read are narratives told from an insider's point of view based on real-life experiences. We solicited these contributions by asking gender scholars to construct cases based on their own scholarly work. While some contributors use actual data from current projects to give "voice" to their cases, others use current examples from the media to provide a context for case construction.

In generating this book, our goal was to "extend the realm of your personal experience by introducing you to situations in context that involve real decisions about important issues that, like life, do not lend themselves to superficial or simple analysis."[1] These "situations in context" are represented as cases; there is a long respected tradition of using narrative to teach and explore "the realities people presuppose in defining themselves and enacting their social and relational identities."[2] You will find both full-length cases as well as shorter "mini-cases" in the book. Full cases more deeply highlight the complexities of gender/ed realities and probably require reading and reflection before class time, while mini-cases can be read either in class or ahead of time and provide a quick touch point for discussion while still being centered in dialogue. In combination, both types of cases provide a unique framework for "actualizing" gender.

ACTUALIZING GENDER: NARRATING A DIALOGUE OF GENDER/ED REALITIES

We have constructed these cases using several insights from narrative theory to help encourage dialoguing about gender/ed realities. To begin, you will notice the characters in these cases talk to each other; we included as much dialogue as possible so it becomes "real" in actualizing gender. This inclusion of dialogue was intentional—a social constructionist perspective toward *communicatively constructing realities* prescribes that our social world is constructed through communication and so the sharing of dialogue is a way to represent that. In other words, it makes sense to highlight communication in the narrative because it is through daily talk that gender/ed realities are (re)produced.

You will also notice the cases are left without complete resolution at a *decision point* (or in simpler terms, unfinished) so that the dialogue is not closed off and the discussion can continue in the classroom through a multiplicity of voices. Leaving cases at a decision point frees you as a learner from trying to find a "correct" outcome, and with this freedom we hope you can fully discuss the various options and potential outcomes that could be taken up at the end of the case with your instructor and peers.

Finally, you will notice that cases are written in ways to illustrate how no narrative ever operates in isolation. Our personal "realities" are shaped by the discourses of institutions in which we participate (including families, organizations, media, religion, etc.) and the societies in which we live. As noted by Lynn Harter, Phyllis Japp, and Christie Beck, "No narrative is solely personal, organizational, or public; stories necessarily bleed across the artificial boundaries of discrete areas of knowledge."[3]

ACTUALIZING GENDER: UNDERSTANDING THE DIALOGUE OF GENDER/ED REALITIES

Now that you understand how narratives can help in dialoguing about gender/ed realities, there are several terms regarding gender that you should understand to fully participate in the dialogue. First, there is the issue of gender/sex and sex/gender; you may have observed that sex is not in our title. We highlight *gender* rather than sex because through these cases we wish to illustrate the social construction of our gender/ed realities rather than place emphases on biological sex.[4] You will notice in the table of contents that we further expand "realities" to gender/ed realities. In choosing this representation, we are trying to illustrate two things. First, we use *gender realities* to highlight that each of us constructs our own gender identity—how we see ourselves as masculine, feminine, and/or androgynous. Second, we use *gendered realities* to highlight how we operate in reference to structures of gender—those institutionalized gender expectations or "rules" that tell us how we should "do gender" in various contexts.

To *actualize*[5] is to make real or concrete, to "give reality or substance to" something. For us, these cases bring to life the sometimes complicated terms and views associated with gender. Thus, our intent is to help you actualize or give substance to the topics you are reading about in your gender course through case studies that illustrate how we communicatively construct gender/ed realities.[6] As noted in Erika and Chad's narrative, "patriarchy" is an important term for understanding gender/ed realities throughout history that can sometimes be hard to discern in everyday life. So reading an example of how Heather negotiates the patriarchy of the Catholic Church in her marriage preparation and through her daily prayer (Mini-case 31) can give substance to your dialogue about the role of patriarchy in gender/ed realities and hopefully make the term "come to life."

When we speak of *communicatively constructing realities,* we are implying a social constructionist view of the world. As previously discussed, this approach examines "reality" not as something that objectively exists, but that instead is subjectively constituted through dialogue (and our reflections upon current dialogue in light of prior dialogue). In this process of social construction, many voices are present. We construct gender/ed realities not only based on personal and relational communication, but also based on how we interact with institutional and cultural/societal discourses. In this communal constitution, each person has a unique view of what reality means to her or him. That's why we have chosen to use *realities* rather than a singular reality, as one reality does not exist.

Finally, we think it is important for you to understand *intersectionality* (of identities and therefore realities) to truly understand the dialogue. Here is an analogy based on Audre Lorde's metaphor of ingredients to aid in your understanding of intersectionality.[7] Think of the multiple facets of your identity—such as sex, gender, race/ethnicity, socio-economic class, sexuality, ability, age, etc.—as colored pencils. If following gender/ed stereotypes, you might color your (biological) sex as pink or blue. Then you decide to represent your (psychological) gender as purple, and color that over the top of your pink or blue. You then find a pencil that is close to the color of your actual skin tone, and add that to the mix. You choose yellow to illustrate your socioeconomic class (etc.). It then occurs to you that you want to concentrate on showing the "purpleness" of your gender (what Lorde would call "plucking out" one aspect of our identity). However, now purple has been combined with pink or blue, a shade of brown, and yellow, so you cannot just take it back out without erasing everything. In more complex terms, the ingredients intersect and are inextricably linked.

Given this notion of *intersectional identities* (e.g., multiple ingredients of identity that are pre-combined and linked), our gender/ed identity will influence our gender/ed realities because identity impacts how we see ourselves in relation to others (and how we are seen) in our world. We learn from an early age that the ingredients of our identity have different expectations and stereotypes placed upon them. So when Lorde discusses her experiences as African-American, female, and lesbian, each ingredient places her in a unique social space, and when combined she has the possibility for multiple forms of oppression (or emancipation, depending on whether one is of the dominant group). We tried to highlight the complexities of intersectionality throughout these cases to further deepen your discussions of gender/ed realities.

ACTUALIZING GENDER: ORGANIZING THE DIALOGUE OF GENDER/ED REALITIES

In talking about how to organize this book, we considered several alternatives, but ultimately chose to take a grounded theory approach and "code" the cases for themes so as not to force cases into any pre-existing context (e.g., gender in education, gender in organizations, etc.). For each case and mini-case, we noted the action that was happening via the characters in relation to gender, and after several iterations, came to agreement that as gender was "actualized," six types of action emerged in relation to gender/ed realities:

1. personalizing↔politicizing
2. (re)acting
3. (re)creating
4. (re)evaluating
5. reproducing↔challenging
6. (re)positioning

While arguments could be made for some cases and mini-cases to be in more than one section, we felt this organizational scheme allowed us to highlight the *process* of actualizing gender in daily life.

As we were inspired by dialogue in constructing the narratives, so were we in labeling these categories of gender/ed action. Mikhail Bahktin noted that no word represents a term, relationship, or situation in one singular way, but rather, you can have seemingly opposite words that both describe the theme in a new way.[8] As we were developing our categories, this notion became particularly clear. We know that gender/ed realities are usually complicated, messy, and ongoing, so we did not want to make the section titles seem final. Instead, we wanted to acknowledge complexity by using words with duality to (again) highlight the *process* of actualizing gender in daily life.

The first set of cases in the book *personalize↔politicize gender/ed realities.* "The personal is the political" was a mantra of second-wave feminism that recognizes that any political action (no matter how seemingly grandiose) has personal consequences. Further, our daily personal lives can serve to reinforce or challenge larger political acts. Our first unit of cases highlights this connection between the personal and political worlds. For example, Teresa Gomez embodies the intersection of the political (i.e., immigration policy) and the personal as she decides whether she should take her children back to Mexico or leave them in the United States after she and her husband are arrested in a raid for "illegal immigrants" (Case 1).

The second set of cases illustrate people *(re)acting amidst gender/ed realities*. In our daily lives, there are times where the circumstances "are what they are," and we must find a way to operate within those circumstances. In other words, we may have to act or react to a situation that we may not like. While we may want to challenge or react to gender/ed realities, other times we have to act within these gender structures. One case representing this gender/ed (re)action is that of Brett, a new college student who feels pressure to perform masculinity in a very narrow way at State University through drinking and being a "player," and therefore has to decide how he wants to negotiate his performance of masculinity (Case 6).

In the third section, the individuals in the cases are *(re)creating gender/ed realities* in light of having a major life change (i.e., adopting, stay-at-home parenting, disability, sex reassignment, etc.). These cases highlight the power we have to create (and recreate) gendered identities for ourselves and others, illustrating that identity is never completely fixed or static. An exemplar is the case of Kay, the mother of a Chinese daughter who is faced with the dilemma of how to explain to her daughter that girls in China are less valued than baby boys while not threatening her daughter's identity as both a girl and someone born in China (Case 12).

The fourth set of cases show individuals who feel a need to *(re)evaluate gender/ed realities*. In these cases, the characters are stuck at a crossroads (i.e., negotiating parenting, marriage, work-life balance, etc.) and must evaluate and reevaluate what their decision means for their gender/ed reality. A case representing this gender/ed (re)evaluation is that of Dan and Tony, a gay couple who are foster parenting a young African-American girl and struggle with the question of whether two white men can successfully parent an African American girl when the option to adopt her becomes available (Case 18).

In the cases of section five, individuals are taking actions that *reproduce↔challenge gender/ed realities*. These cases highlight the intersection of gender/ed identity with larger social networks and systems. The characters in these cases are facing the decision of whether or not to reproduce gender/ed realities through silence or to resist this reproduction and instead challenge the members of their social networks through conversation. As an example of such a decision, Sarah is a college professor who lives separately from her husband during the work week, and when people in her small town start gossiping about their marriage breaking up, she and her husband must decide how to deal with the gossip (Case 24).

The sixth and final set of cases are those that *(re)position gender/ed realities.* In these cases, the main characters reflect on how to position (and reposition) themselves or the organizations of which they are a part within a particular gender/ed context. This positioning may be a gendered identity they want to move toward [e.g., OSCLG (Organization for the Study of Communication, Language, and Gender) and the YWCA as feminist organizations] or move away from (e.g., a parent who re-inscribes gendered roles through toys). As one example, when Jake is confronted by his male friends after his wife kicks him out of the house, he says he "only" yelled and threw something at her—but did not hit her— and so resists the label of "abuser" and attempts to reposition his identity for himself and others (Case 29).

Taken together, these 34 cases/mini-cases provide many examples to foster a dialogue about gender/ed realities. The next step is up to you and how you engage the material.

ACTUALIZING GENDER: PARTICIPATING IN THE DIALOGUE OF GENDER/ED REALITIES

While these cases were constructed with the power of narrative in mind, the real impact relies on you as a community of learners. As Mikhail Bahktin noted, "the living utterance, having taken meaning and shape at a particular historical moment in a socially specific environment, cannot fail to brush up against thousands of living dialogic threads, woven by socio-ideological consciousness around the given object of utterance."[9] In other words, the dialogue we and our contributors have created was in a particular time and place, but our words live on through you and your interpretations of the cases and their relationship to gender. It is up to you to contribute to the dialogue about gender/ed realities and help bring these gender terms and issues to life. After all, words are just words unless we create meaning through dialogue.

Philosopher Kenneth Burke talked about creating a community of dialogue in a slightly different way. Burke used the term "unending conversation"[10] to describe a party scene where you walk in and hear a lively discussion. The discussion began long before your arrival, and no one at the party can tell you all of the points of the discussion, so you start by listening to what is being said. As you start to feel more comfortable with the terms and arguments, you can "dip your oar" into the conversation and start explaining your thoughts about what is being discussed. Even though the discussion will continue after you leave the party, your contributions impacted the dialogue.

Bahktin and Burke help us frame how we hope you will use this collection. Well before us, scholars and others have discussed, debated, and co-constructed these gender/ed terms and realities. Just because these terms are in a book does not mean the discussion is over. Rather, think of yourself as joining us at our party in midstream. As you study gender throughout this course, try dipping your oar into the discussion. It is our hope that these cases will provide a context for all who encounter them to become a part of a larger dialogue about gender/ed realities.

endnotes

1. Delaat, J., Hawthorne, E. M., & Schroer-Lamont. (n.d., ¶ 1) *Case studies on gender issues in the workplace—Results of an interactive workshop.* Retrieved September 24, 2007 from http://www.agecon.uga.edu/~wacra/gend-luc.htm

2. Harter, L. M., Japp, P., & Beck, C. (2005, p. 10). *Narratives, health, and healing: Communication theory, research and practice.* Mahwah, NJ: Lawrence Erlbaum.

3. Harter, Japp, and Beck (2005, p. 8).

4. Of course, we do recognize that people are often identified and interacted with based on their biological sex, feeding back into gender.

5. actualize. (n.d.). Princeton University's WordNet® 3.0. Retrieved September 12, 2008 from Dictionary.com website: http://dictionary.reference.com/browse/actualize

6. The index cross references common gender course topics with relevant cases for instructors and students to choose which cases are best suited for discussing a certain gender/ed idea.

7. Lorde, A. (1984). *Sister outsider.* Trumansberg, NY: The Crossing Press.

8. Bahktin, M. M. (1981). *The dialogic imagination: Four essays by M. M. Bahktin* (M. Holquist, Ed.; C. Emerson & M. Holquist, Trans.). Austin: University of Texas Press.

9. Bahktin (1981, p. 276).

10. Burke, K. (1941/1973). *The philosophy of literary form.* Berkeley: University of California Press.

PERSONALIZING↔POLITICIZING GENDER/ED REALITIES

introduction

The cases in this section *personalize↔politicize gender/ed realities.* "The personal is the political" was a mantra of second-wave feminism that recognizes that any political action (no matter how seemingly grandiose) has personal consequences. Further, our daily personal lives can serve to reinforce or challenge larger political acts. These cases highlight this connection between the personal and political worlds.

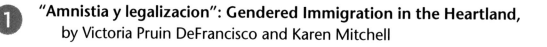

1   "Amnistia y legalizacion": Gendered Immigration in the Heartland, by Victoria Pruin DeFrancisco and Karen Mitchell

2   "What Do You Mean 'Just a Girl?'": Sergeant Stiles and a Media-Military Crisis, by John W. Howard III and Laura C. Prividera

3   "Being Homeless and Gay or Lesbian is a Difficult Combination": An Invisible Population, by Renee Houston

4   To Guard or Not Guard?: Dilemmas Surrounding the Human Papillomavirus Vaccine, by Marie Thompson and Lynn M. Harter

5   "Heaping Hostility on Hillary": "Isms" in the 2008 Presidential Race, by Lynn H. Turner and Patricia A. Sullivan

"Amnistia y legalizacion"
Gendered Immigration in the Heartland

Victoria Pruin DeFrancisco
and Karen Mitchell

For Teresa Gómez[1], the past few months had been a nightmare. The Postville immigration raid seemed like yesterday. She had feared being arrested but never thought her family would be torn apart. Father Bill had suggested she seek help from Catholic Charities, which is why she found herself standing outside the building today. She walked in and was directed to the office of Julia, a social services provider with the agency. Teresa settled into a sofa in the office and introduced herself. "Soy Teresa Gómez. Soy de Petapa, Guatemala. Tengo 33 años. Mi marido, Víctor yo llegamos a Postville, Iowa hace 11 años. Tenemos two hijos, Olivia de nine años y Vicente, que tiene seven años. No hablo mucho inglés, pero quiero que sepan mi historia. El padre Bill dice que son buena gente, ¿no?"[2]

"Welcome, Teresa. Yes, I am a person you can trust, and I want to help you if I can. Let's start with you telling me about yourself and your family," said Julia.

"Teresa is not my real name. I was born Antonia Montoya Saché. I came to the United States 12 years ago to find work. I can make more money here than at home. In Petapa, I worked in an office and liked it very much, but I could not make enough money to live on. I decided to come to America with my friend Rosa to make money to send to my family. I would work hard and become a U.S. citizen, buy a big house, and one day my parents would come join me. This is the American dream, I thought."

"I can't imagine leaving was easy for you," comforted Julia.

"Papá wept the day I left Petapa. 'Come back to us soon, little sparrow,' he whispered. I closed my eyes to hold back the tears as he kissed my cheek. I did not know then that I would never see his kind eyes again. Papá died five years ago. Mamá is alone now, and in every letter she writes, 'When will you come home, chita? I want to see my grandchildren before I, too, die.' I tell her 'Pronto, Mamá, muy pronto,' but everything costs so much here. We cannot save many dollars. It makes my heart sick to think of home. I miss the warm sun. Iowa is so cold in the winter; my blood does not get thick in the winter like some people. I miss my family. I miss the beautiful land, the food . . . fish, elote, and yucca that Mamá and the other women in the neighborhood would prepare in our kitchen. I miss the nightly community get-togethers. When you had a problem everyone would try to help. You were never alone.

"But I made my mind up to go to the United States. Traveling here was not easy. It was a long and difficult trip—over a month, mostly walking. Even though I had a temporary visa that allowed me to enter the country legally, I was afraid. My friend Rosa and I had jobs picking oranges in Florida, but we got paid very little, and when the season ended we didn't have enough money to return home if we had wanted to. We met a man who lived in Iowa and was looking for workers. He told us about good paying jobs at meat packing plants with housing provided, so Rosa and I agreed to come here."

"What was it like for you once you got here?" Julia asked.

"I worked on an assembly line pulling the feathers off chickens when they came out of a steaming vat of water. It was very hot, and we were crowded together. Sometimes the heat and the smells of the plant made my stomach churn so much that I would taste stomach acid in my mouth, but I needed the money, so I never complained. There were supervisors who watched to see if we were working fast enough and getting the birds' skin clean. 'Faster, María! You are slowing-up the line!' my supervisor would scream. 'My name is not María. I am Antonia.' 'Whatever . . . you wetbacks are all the same to me. Just move your ass!'

" 'Se cree que soy un burro,' I would whisper to myself in Spanish. I wore a white apron, hat and mask, but still I went home with the smell of cooked feathers on my hair and skin. No matter how much I bathed or how long I scrubbed, I could not remove the stink. The women at the plant gave me soaps and sprays, but nothing worked. Never would I attract a man and have a family of my own if I smelled like scorched feathers. 'Wear more makeup,' the Latino women at the plant would tell me, 'and the men will smell only the sex!' they would joke, but I did not laugh at their vulgar thoughts. I felt only shame.

"The job paid $6.75 an hour, which in Petapa is a great deal of money, but in Iowa it is not so much. And I never got the free housing I was promised. Rosa and I were lonely, and missed our home and our families. After six months Rosa returned to Petapa, but I didn't want to disappoint my parents and decided to stay."

"I can understand that," Julia sympathized. "Were there any legal issues with you staying in the country longer?"

"The laws for immigrants in this country are very confusing," Teresa said. "When my temporary visa expired, I asked for an extension, but I was denied. The man at work gave me a new name, Teresa Gómez, and a number that he said would allow me to stay in Iowa and continue to work. I knew this was wrong, but how else could I send Mamá and Papá money? And then I met my husband, Víctor Tajaj Sologûi."

"Oh yeah?" said Julia. "How did you meet him, Antonia?"

"Sandra, a friend at St. Bridget's Catholic Church, introduced me to Víctor the first summer I was in Iowa. Usually the men don't go to church much; it is a place more for the women to gather, but Víctor is a man of faith. He was from my city, and together we talked of home. He worked at the same plant and soon we were spending much time together. Courtship is very different to us than for Americans. Víctor and I married quickly to begin our family. My wedding was simple, with only a few friends present. Father Bill married us at St. Bridget's on October 14, 1997. 'Someday we will marry again with our family surrounding us and a wedding feast to follow,' Víctor told me that night as we lay in our wedding bed. 'Some day when we are home . . .'

"At first, Víctor made more money than I did because he could do the heavier work," Teresa continued. "He cut the loins off the cows. The knife was very sharp, and the work was hard. He would bring the knife home every day to sharpen, and I warned him, 'You will cut yourself.'

" 'Teresa, a sharp knife makes my job easier. My arm gets so tired—up and cut down, up and cut down—over and over again, eight hours a day. You like the money I make? Stop worrying,' he laughed.

"Then one day, just after our son started second grade, Víctor's knife slipped, and he severed the tendons in his right hand. He almost lost the use of his hand, and for months he struggled to do even simple movements. At first I thought we might get extra money because Víctor was hurt at work, but the plant's insurance company denied our claim: 'Safety instructions were clearly posted in the immediate work area,' the letter said. Too bad instructions were posted only in English."

"How did you make ends meet with only one income?" asked Julia.

"I was lucky to be healthy and strong enough to work extra hours while he recovered," Teresa explained, "but I often returned home from work too tired and sore to care for our children. Those were bad times, with little money and no hope for the future, but God provided enough for us. When Víctor returned to work, he could no longer work with the men, so he took a lower paying job like mine, working with the women. We couldn't afford childcare, and we have no family here, so Víctor worked nights, and I worked days.

"Víctor is a good father, a kind man with a gentle soul. He took extra shifts when he could to put food on the table. Our friends look to him for advice, and he is loved by many in our pueblo. He is a man of very few words, and since his English is not so good, I am the one who talks to the teachers about Olivia and Vicente's school work. The children, she told me, are bright and very talented. 'Give them extra help in reading,' she said, but I cannot read English so well myself. I asked the padre for help, and he spends time reading with Olivia and working math problems with Vicente. When the children receive high marks in school, Father Bill lets them play on the computer in the rectory. These were happy times for my children."

"Go on . . ." encouraged Julia.

"Life for us was finally getting better until this spring. The day was Monday, May 12. Victor's supervisor asked him to work a double shift. My friend Sandra offered to watch the children. I had just finished my break when suddenly there were many, many men carrying guns, running everywhere and yelling 'Freeze!' I didn't know what was happening. A kidnapping or something? It was violent. Someone screamed, 'Redada! ICE! Run!' We scattered as best we could, like rabbits, falling and stumbling in a panic to hide. I was in a hallway and had nowhere to run. I was caught right away. They pushed me against the wall and held me there, yelling in English, 'Drop to your knees! Don't try to fight!' Some workers hid in meat lockers, freezers, bathroom stalls, or under stacks of cardboard boxes. One woman near me hid in a mound of chicken feathers; they say another hid in a tub of blood and guts."

Julia just shook her head in horror.

"They arrested nearly 400 of us Latino immigrant workers. They loaded us on buses like cattle and took us out of town. We were in a make-shift jail with rows and rows of cots, surrounded by wire fences. The bathrooms were filthy, and there was no privacy. At first, I could not find Víctor. I prayed he had escaped and was hiding with our children at the church. He was not so lucky. Both of us were charged with something—'aggravated identity theft.' We are poor people, hard working; neither of us had ever been arrested before.

"Víctor is in a jail now, but I don't know where. Some say in Louisiana. I wear a GPS chain on my ankle so the police know where I am. The police split many, many families that day. No one seems to care. Who knows when—or if—we will be reunited. They let me and many other mothers go because there was no one to care for our children, but I am under house arrest. It shames me that my children see me with ankle chains. I am not allowed to work. I worry we will soon be homeless. The children cry for their father; they are hungry for food; they fear I will disappear again, and they will be alone. The padre is searching to find information about Víctor, but so far, we know nothing."

"How are your children?" asked Julia.

"I try to soothe the children, but I wait in fear. The authorities say it may be six months before I will have a hearing. They will fine me money I do not have. I will likely go to jail again and then be deported. Who will watch my children then? My friend Sandra says if I can get the money for a plane ticket, I could return home voluntarily, instead of having an official deportation on my record, which would prevent me from re-entering the United States for years. But where am I going to get the money for tickets? I need to stay here. My children were born here; they speak English. They are U.S. citizens. This is the only home they know. They speak only a little Spanish; they have mostly American friends. This is not fair to them. For the children of illegals, there is no American dream.

"Sometimes I wish I could run. Father Bill told me about a woman in Chicago whose priest hid her and her children in a church for over a year." Teresa continued. "Her name was Elvira Arellano, and she was safe until she decided to speak out about her treatment. Once she left the safety of her church, she was arrested and deported. Her children were placed in foster care. She is only one of many deportees. Some Latino immigrants who have lived here since they were babies were deported, forced to return to a place they do not know.

"I am a woman with two children, alone. I don't understand English very well, and now I have no way to earn a living. It is a humid, hot summer, and I am afraid to go out. I peek out at the empty street from behind a blue bed sheet I hung over the picture window because of my shame and fear. We'll stay hidden in our small apartment until the landlord kicks us out. At night I lay in bed reliving what happened to us, over and over."

"I can't even imagine . . ." whispered Julia.

"Lately, I've been thinking the unthinkable. Would my children be better off staying here without me? The United States is their home. Here they could get good educations, graduate from high school, maybe go to college. They'd have opportunities for better lives. My friend Sandra loves my babies. Maybe she would keep them here until I can return. But who am I kidding? How many years might pass before I could be reunited with my children . . . my husband? It was my plan to bring my parents to America; look at how that worked out. I have learned that days pass slowly when separated from loved ones.

"In my Latino culture, to split the family is a grievous sin that one should never consider. But, the U.S. government split my family, and I split my family 12 years ago when I left Petapa. I just don't know what I should do now . . . ¿Qué hacemos? ¿Qué hacemos?"

endnotes

1. This is a narrative of Antonia Montoya Saché's experience in the United States as a so-called illegal immigrant. It focuses around events that took place in Postville, Iowa, in 2008, to bring attention to the personal consequences of what was called the largest immigration raid in the history of the United States. Antonia's experience represents the experiences of many immigrants without official papers. Her story is drawn from a compilation of interviews with Latino immigrants from Guatemala, Mexico, and El Salvador; interviews with social service providers and clergy serving immigrants in northeastern Iowa; from newspaper and academic research reports; and finally, our own opportunities along with our students to become acquainted with the more recent residents of Iowa.

2. We chose not to translate all the Spanish and native language phrases from Western Guatemala (Quiché). These not only add to the authenticity of many Latino immigrants' perspectives presented here, but they also provide small glimpses of what it is like to be left out of communication due to language barriers. Special thanks for Spanish and Quiché language and cultures expertise from Jennifer Cooley, Ph.D., Associate Professor, Department of Modern Languages, University of Northern Iowa.

"What Do You Mean 'Just a Girl?'"

Sergeant Stiles and a Media-Military Crisis

John W. Howard III
and Laura C. Prividera

It had been a hectic two weeks for the U.S. Army division headquarters. Military progress had recently been slow and the suppression of Iraqi insurgents was not only unsuccessful, but the number of attacks on U.S. military personnel had increased exponentially in the past two months. As a public affairs staffer, Sergeant Sharon Stiles had been in charge of sharing that information directly with media representatives. However, an even more sensational story had recently been unfolding. It had been discovered that a number of U.S. soldiers were involved in the mistreatment and abuse of detainees in their care.[1] It was a certainty that the impending public airing of this story would aggravate problems with soldier morale and waning public support for military involvement in Iraq. Thus, she faced a serious challenge today in formulating her position on how to frame this for the media and, ultimately, the U.S. public.

Sergeant Stiles stared at her computer monitor and wondered, "How could such a mess have happened, and how would it impact the day-to-day challenges of maintaining a good public image for the United States' oldest military institution?" She had been a spokesperson for the Army division office for five years, and nothing like this had ever happened before. In her 10 years of experience working for the Army, she had to speak to many tragic, intense, graphic, and troubling issues, but none of it prepared her for the crisis she was now facing. She reviewed the events as summarized in the military's investigatory report.

The investigation revealed that a unit of military police had been mistreating detainees over the past six months in the "Shelter A" holding area.[2] Shelter A was reserved for detainees who had suspected links to terrorism or insurgent activities against the armed forces. Early in the war, the President's office had suspended the Geneva Conventions for the detainees because they were perceived as potential "terrorists" rather than "prisoners of war." The goal was to open opportunities for military intelligence (MI) to gather information. As it turned out, more than 90 percent of the detainees were innocent men, women, and children who had no connections with terrorist or insurgent activity—a finding that had been creating profound tensions between the U.S. military and the civilian Iraqi population.

Shelter A was physically and administratively separate from other prisons and detainee holding centers. The military police (MP) unit in charge of the facility was a reserve unit and not trained in corrections or intelligence work. Yet, military investigations revealed that the MP unit was often answering directly to members of the MI unit and other high-ranking administrative units charged with obtaining information. The lack of appropriate training and the involvement of MPs in assisting in intelligence gathering undermined MP credibility and obfuscated the ethical standards to which they were expected to adhere.

In addition, the investigation found that the chain of command was ambiguous and contributed to the abuse. The soldiers questioned in the investigation witnessed the commanding officer of the MP unit, Sergeant Tim Vascar, being told by MI to "do whatever it takes" to prepare detainees for interrogations. Various members of the MP unit participated in the "softening" of detainees, which included a variety of techniques to emotionally, mentally, and physically exhaust them before they were questioned. At the direction of Sergeant Vascar, many U.S. soldiers used strategies included stripping detainees of their clothes, keeping them in uncomfortable environments, embarrassing/humiliating them and their culture, and preventing them from sleeping for extended periods. Soldiers had seen MI superiors praise Sergeant Vascar for his efforts—efforts that were photographed, videotaped, and passed along to numerous military personnel. The images were disturbing. Many showed detainees naked and posed in degrading or sexually compromising positions.

An even more troubling element of the photos was the inclusion of one or more U.S. soldiers as they participated in the abuse. The most memorable photographs were of a lesser involved unit clerk, Private Melisa Angler. In one photo, Private Angler was pictured laughing as she pointed at a naked detainee's genitalia. In another photo, she held a "leash" attached to a detainee who was on his hands and knees as if he were a pet on a walk. The photos pictured Private Angler at the center of these events. However, witnesses indicated that she was ordered by Sergeant Vascar, her superior officer, to appear in the photos because her sex would humiliate the detainees. It was widely known that the detainees were uncomfortable around women, particularly when they were unclothed. Private Angler reportedly complied with Sergeant Vascar's requests as he was her superior officer, and surrounding MI personnel indicated they were getting the needed information.

A significant amount of media pressure had been put on the Army to publicly reveal the activities at Shelter A. Reports had leaked about mistreatment and the demands for answers were getting louder and louder. In less than an hour, Sergeant Stiles would take part in a meeting with other representatives and officers to discuss how to go about releasing the information to the public. She re-opened the confidential envelope that enclosed the proposal drafted by Major Joseph Thomas, the lead public affairs officer, to read through it once more.

Sergeant Stiles perused the document and supporting materials and paused for a moment, looking absently around the room as she strove for clarity. She pondered, "As written, Major Thomas' proposal turns the focus onto the unilateral actions of the soldiers and, in particular, the activities of Private Angler. He is suggesting using the more dramatic and visually striking dimensions of the story, primarily those of Private Angler, to draw the focus off the military as an institution and place it on individuals since media coverage is often sensationalized." She thought, "This is a clever image-repair strategy that will be well-received by government officials, military personnel, and the public. After all, since the public continues to debate women's participation in the military, this material would clearly incite such dialogues and shift the story's focus as intended." Sergeant Stiles reflected that in spite of being granted official membership in the U.S. military with the passage of the Women's Armed Service Integration Act in 1948, women remain excluded from combat roles. This policy opened many career avenues for her personally, yet combat restrictions also impacted her career path.

Sergeant Stiles then turned to the contents of General Marty Taggert's official investigation report on the events in Shelter A.[3] The General's treatment of the case was comprehensive and direct. It identified numerous cases of abuse and mistreatment and named the soldiers involved. The report certainly would not be the last on the subject, particularly in light of the impending legal action against the soldiers. However, it was also an official review of military practice and policy at Shelter A. She reviewed his summation of the factors that contributed to the mistreatment of the detainees, including:

1. The use of a Military Police unit to act as corrections officers without sufficient training.
2. An inadequate staff to manage such a large population of detainees.
3. A doctrinally unsound command structure that placed the MPs under the direction of Military Intelligence, civilian contractors, and other governmental agencies.
4. A supervisory structure that was lax and did not promote professionalism in the ranks.
5. Poor living and supply conditions that contributed to a low morale among the soldiers.

However, these systemic problems in General Taggert's report were not addressed in the proposed strategy for addressing the crisis. Sergeant Stiles wondered to herself, "How can this be? How can we overlook significant communication and organizational flaws and shift the responsibility to a few soldiers without context?" Sergeant Stiles considered what her job was in public affairs: to represent the Army well to the public and the media. Clearly, shifting the burden directly to the soldiers, with specific attention on Private Angler, relieved the Army of some responsibility in the eyes of the viewer. However, she found such a construction of events unsettling. She wondered, "Is this proposal using sex as a scapegoat?" Certainly, there would be intense discussion today among the public affairs personnel as they worked through these issues.

Sergeant Stiles had many disagreements with supervisors over the years regarding the presentation and use of materials and facts. More than once, she had been involved in heated arguments among colleagues. Public affairs did not lend itself to a cookie-cutter approach to presenting information, but that is what she liked about her job. What happened was often less important than how it was presented and how the organization responded and appeared. It was, without a doubt, an uncertain enterprise.

As she reflected on her past decisions, Sergeant Stiles considered what her mentors had said to her over the years. In her first crisis event, she remembered writing about several soldiers killed in a training exercise. It was a terrible story and there were many mistakes made by the soldiers in the process. When she asked how to best draft the press release, her boss at the time, Sergeant Marissa Green, simply said, "Sharon, your job is to put our best foot forward. It isn't to interrogate. It isn't to fabricate. How can you do that?" Marissa was a soldier of principle, and she trusted the organization she had dedicated her life to serving.

Sergeant Stiles spun her chair around and looked out the window. She could see the flag flying in front of the building. More than a decade ago, she took her oath to "support and defend the Constitution" and to "bear true faith and allegiance to the same." She wondered, "What was the best way to serve in this instance?"

One of her regular collaborators was another seasoned public affairs specialist, Sergeant Jack Burns. She looked at his empty desk and pondered his take on the situation. Sergeant Burns had collaborated with her off and on over the last 18 months as they delivered release after release regarding military progress. Sergeant Burns was a believer in what he called "the greater good." His litmus test for framing events always came back to "what does the most good for the majority?" His thinking generally led him to support framings that upheld military policy, image, and integrity. For Sergeant Burns, public affairs stories were about showcasing Army values and strengths, not disclosing flaws or failings. In particular, he had a distaste for stories about soldier mistakes and indiscretions that he felt constituted "sensationalism and drama." He made it a flat policy not to include either in the documents he prepared. Sergeant Stiles recalled him stating that "women are assets to the military. What would we do without their assistance as nurses, secretaries, cooks, and clerks?" Sergeant Burns would be at the meeting and was reviewing the same materials at the moment.

"Hi Sergeant Stiles." She snapped out of her deep contemplation to see Major Joseph Thomas walk over to her desk.

"Good morning, Major," she replied at attention.

"At ease, soldier." He smiled and made himself a seat at the desk across from her. "I just wanted to see if you'd had a chance to look over the proposal yet."

"Absolutely, sir." She paused, "I was just reflecting on it."

"Good!" said Major Thomas. "This is the most important media issue we've had to handle in a number of years—I don't want to screw it up."

"Of course not," Sergeant Stiles replied. They made eye contact for a few moments. Sergeant Stiles had known the Major only a short time. He was recognized for his good humor and likability. However, in the same breath, people would note his impatience for disagreement, particularly if he thought he was in the right. Major Thomas would be one of the people at the meeting and would have a significant say regarding how and by whom the story would be handled.

Major Thomas broke the silence as they stared at one another, "Sharon, I think we have an opportunity here to make or break the public faith in our mission. As we all know, some dimensions of this conflict are not progressing as we'd like. It is hard on soldier morale and civilian confidence in our efforts here and at home. I think the proposal drafted does an excellent job of disclosing mistakes that were made without creating undue loss of faith in the military organization we have vowed to serve." He paused for a moment then continued, "I hate to see soldiers do bad things. It runs contrary to our oath and our purpose. But I don't think the events here should be allowed to tarnish the institution's reputation. Besides, these were the acts of some careless individuals and of one in particular in the pictures. She's just a misguided girl—not at all representative of what the Army stands for."

Sergeant Stiles nodded, "I see, sir."

"Good! Then I'll see you at the meeting in 30 minutes!" She started to rise as he did and Major Thomas put his hand out and smiled, "sit back down, soldier. There will be plenty of formalities in a half hour."

Sergeant Stiles watched as he swiftly strode out of the room and wondered, "Did I just give him my approval to scapegoat the soldiers in this event? Did I just sell one of them out because she is female? 'Just a girl?' Isn't she a soldier?" Her stomach started to turn.

She flipped through the proposal and supporting materials again. It eloquently described the events. It also squarely seated blame on the soldiers with a large focus on Private Melisa Angler, who was featured in nearly all of the supporting photographs to be released. More than 250 photographs were confiscated but only a dozen were to be made available to the public. Access was restricted to all of the photos, a decision made by those directly working on the proposal. As Sergeant Stiles read, she replayed a conversation she had overheard among some officers the previous day: "'You know, that is just another reason why women shouldn't be in the field. They do crazy things. That Angler character is making all of us look bad. She probably made Vascar crazy and increased his workload.' 'Now Charlie,' replied the other, 'that isn't entirely true. She was not the only one.' 'Look at the pictures,' Charlie responded, 'The proof is right there. She's the center of it all.' 'Well' the officer paused, 'you have a point. This wouldn't be such a big deal if it wasn't a *she*. She is a media disaster for the military. That's why they are not allowed in combat. Imagine what we'd have to deal with then.'"

She had experienced such disparagement of women in the military since before she enlisted. "It was a man's job," her father insisted, "no place for little girls." Her mother, though supportive, warned against "entering a man's world" because "you can get hurt." As she moved through the ranks and saw her own advancement and the advancement of others, she was frequently reminded of the masculine nature of the military. The songs they sang in training, the images of the "warrior hero" protecting "the motherland," pervasive sexual humor and gendered language, and frequent references to men's strength and women's weakness all reminded Sergeant Stiles of how hard she worked to assimilate into a masculine world.

Sergeant Stiles mentally recited the statistics she used in her promotional materials and speaking engagements: "Women's presence in the U.S. military has steadily increased over the past three decades, from 3 percent in 1972 to 14.6 percent active duty personnel in 2005. And, at present, women comprised 14 percent of the Army, 6 percent of Marines, 14 percent of the Navy, and 20 percent of the Air Force."[4] Yet, women are still a minority of military representatives and remain excluded from many jobs because of their sex. Sergeant Stiles began to think of the significance of how the story "spin" may affect not only the military but women's uncertain status in it. It occurred to her that this was yet one more decision where sex was playing a role in the final outcome.

The meeting was in 10 minutes, so Sergeant Stiles assembled her materials and placed them in her portfolio. More than two dozen people would be there to address the crisis and discuss the viability of the preliminary proposal. After they developed a response, it would be sent to other officers and government officials for final delivery to the public and media representatives. But the process would start today. She began to think what opposing the proposal would mean for her future career advancement. She wondered about her own sex and how that would influence her peers and superiors' perceptions and responses to her concerns. She wondered, "Really, what should I say? Do I promote the use of a female soldier as a shield for bigger issues? How do I do what I believe is right?" Closing the office door, she did not have clear answers but she knew they would have to come before she reached the end of the hall.

endnotes

1. This case is based on media coverage of actual events; however names and places have been altered and several roles have been dramatized.
2. Hersh, S. (2004, May 10). Torture at Abu Ghraib. *The New Yorker, 80* (11), 42–47.
3. Taguba, A. (2004, March 9). Article 15-6 investigation of the 800th military police brigade. U.S. Washington, DC: U.S. Department of Defense.
4. U.S. Department of Defense. (2006). Active duty military personnel by rank/grade (for September 30, 2005). www.dior.whs.mil/mmid/military/history/rg0109f.pdf

"Being Homeless and Gay or Lesbian Is a Difficult Combination"

An Invisible Population

Renee Houston

KEY TERMS

- heteronormativity
- stereotypes
- homophobia
- inclusiveness

As the principal investigator of a community-wide project to combat homelessness, Alexa often found herself meeting with directors of social service organizations in order to create opportunities to interview their clients who were experiencing homelessness. It was the second year of the project and all of the materials, plans, and questions for the survey were refined and approved by her university's review board. The project itself had led her to think more broadly about what was important to her in the community. She now often found herself saying that "The measure of a good community is how it treats those who are most in need."

In conversation with friends and family she found herself doing a lot of educating about the issues surrounding homelessness. She thought to herself, "I used to be one of those people that thought solving homelessness was as simple as people getting a job to get off the streets. But now I know it is about substance abuse, mental health, disabilities, domestic violence, and the like. It is much more of a complex problem than at first blush, and many more people are affected by it than I originally realized."

On this particular day she was headed for her first meeting with an agency she had not yet partnered with. "I hope Marla was right that this Executive Director is supportive of the work and will be willing to help me coordinate with the case managers to make arrangements for interviews with families who are experiencing homelessness," Alexa hoped. As she exited her car, Alexa felt this meeting would be an important one since it would introduce an often hidden population to the community: families experiencing homelessness. Unlike the urban homeless who were mainly single white men, families were not easy to find and many community members did not realize that almost 50 percent of the homeless population were families. Their voices were important to her research.

At the start of the meeting, the Executive Director praised Alexa for her past research efforts and her commitment to helping the community understand homelessness. During the meeting, many of the case managers asked important logistical questions: "How should they offer to include their clients? Where would the interviews be conducted? Could working people be accommodated after 5 P.M.?" As the meeting hummed along, Alexa was energized by their informed questions and willingness to help solve problems to include their important population of families experiencing homelessness.

The group continued to ask logistical questions and offer assistance for meeting with their client families. One case manager who had been a little quiet spoke up, "How are you going to include gay and lesbian individuals who are experiencing homelessness? While less than 10 percent of Americans label themselves as gay or lesbian, upwards of 40 percent of the homeless youth identify as LGBT[1] (lesbian–gay–bisexual–transgender). One report cites that half of gay teens report a negative reaction from their family, and 26 percent of them are actually kicked out of the house.[2] They are never going to show up in shelters—shelters are dangerous places for them because if they are known as LGBT they will be ostracized at best, but usually end up beaten and abused. As a result, many of them go underground to places where you won't find them. Being homeless and gay or lesbian is a difficult combination. Do you even ask questions about sexuality in your interviews?"

Alexa found herself becoming flushed and embarrassed. She thanked the case manager for the thoughtful questions and information and told her that she would consult with her research team about what could be done. She left the meeting frustrated with herself. In her attempt to include everyone, she had overlooked an invisible population that was a much-needed voice in the community. How had she overlooked this intersection in the homeless community? She could not imagine a family forcing a child to move out of the house and into the streets. What could she do now to make sure their voices were heard? She had reflected earlier in the day that "the measure of a good community is how it treats those who are most in need," so how could the community best respond to the needs of this youth population?

endnotes

1. LGBT (also GLBT): either of these expressions are acronyms for individuals who are lesbian, gay, bisexual, or transgender/transsexual. The acronym differs across organizations; for example, the Human Rights Campaign (HRC) utilizes GLBT while the Gay, Lesbian and Straight Education Network (GLSEN) utilizes LGBT.
2. Ray, N. (2006). Lesbian, gay, bisexual, and transgendered youth: An epidemic of homelessness [Report]. National Gay and Lesbian Task Force Policy Institute & National Coalition of the Homeless from http://www.thetaskforce.org/downloads/HomelessYouth.pdf

To Guard or Not Guard?

Dilemmas Surrounding the Human Papillomavirus Vaccine

Marie Thompson and Lynn M. Harter

KEY TERMS

- ◆ sexual health and medicine
- ◆ heteronormativity
- ◆ institutional power
- ◆ biology
- ◆ inclusiveness

Abby slid behind the wheel of her hybrid Prius, strapped on a seat belt, and put the key in the ignition. Before starting the car, however, she paused to reflect on her recent encounter with Dr. Stacy Smith. Dr. Smith had delivered her and Steve's twins, Ellie and Elijah, 12 years ago, and since that time had served as their family's physician and friend. She had scheduled her appointment with Dr. Smith because of a nasty sinus infection but left with more than a prescription. Abby thumbed through the pamphlet she had taken on Gardasil®, the new vaccine developed by Merck, and recalled Dr. Smith's suggestion to have Ellie vaccinated at her upcoming annual physical. "The reason why I am recommending you consider this for Ellie now is because we can integrate the inoculations as part of the vaccination schedule required for public school attendance for girls entering the sixth grade," Dr. Smith had stressed.

Of course, Abby had heard of Gardasil. It seemed like every time she turned on the television, she saw a commercial encouraging her to have her daughter vaccinated against human papillomavirus (HPV) so that she could grow up to live "one less" life affected by cervical cancer. As she put the car in drive, she thought about how quickly time had passed, "It seems like yesterday that the twins were born, rode the school bus for the first time, and participated in little league soccer, and now the time has come for Steve and me to decide whether

Ellie should be vaccinated for a cancer that arises because of a sexually transmitted virus. Where had time gone?" As Abby drove home, she knew this was not going to be an easy decision.

That evening, Abby and Steve googled to learn more about HPV, cervical cancer, and the development of the Gardasil vaccine to help them make a decision about whether or not to have Ellie vaccinated. They knew from watching the evening news over the past few months that several states were debating proposed legislation that would mandate the Gardasil vaccination for girls prior to junior high. But at this point, in their home state of Ohio, the decision remained a parental one.

Abby and Steve tried to process the multiple screens of information. At WebMD, they learned that cervical cancer is one of the most preventable forms of cancer, and while it is treatable when detected in its early stages, it is the third most prevalent cancer worldwide. It is estimated that nearly 4,000 women will die this year from cervical cancer in the United States alone.

"This equates to 10 deaths every day," mused Steve.

Abby nodded, "What I'm taking from the research reported here is that cervical cancer is pervasive yet preventable, and that it arises from HPV infected tissue."

As Abby and Steve scrolled down the screen, they learned that HPV is a sexually transmitted virus that can remain undetected and/or dormant for over 20 years, and that untreated lesions and ongoing infections associated with four strains of HPV are the primary risk factors leading to cervical cancer. They read that in 2000, the U.S. Congress passed legislation providing monies for ongoing research and increased efforts in prevention and public education about HPV. "I am surprised that people—including us—did not know about the dangers of HPV prior to the Gardasil campaign. I am certainly learning a lot just from our reading tonight," Abby lamented.

Abby and Steve narrowed their search to explore links between the Gardasil vaccine, HPV, and cervical cancer. At the website of the American Cancer Society,[1] they learned Merck had enrolled over 27,000 subjects in 12 separate clinical trials to test the effectiveness of Gardasil since the mid 1990s. Then, in early 2006, Merck petitioned the Food and Drug Administration (FDA) for a priority hearing to approve the implementation of Gardasil due to its impressive clinical trial results and safety in protecting individuals against four types of HPV. After a few more minutes of searching, Abby and Steve found transcripts from the FDA hearing online.[2] "It's amazing how much information is available with just a few clicks of the mouse!" exclaimed Steve.

The FDA's hearing occurred on May 18, 2006 and included representatives from multiple health-related organizations.[3] During the hearing, data was presented illustrating how Gardasil induces an immune response resulting in a 97–99 percent effectiveness rate for the vaccine. Abby exclaimed, "Well, it's about time that public resources and attention are dedicated to women's health issues. The development of this vaccine represents a tremendous scientific break-through that will save the lives of millions of women."

"Wait a second. This is not just about women," stressed Steve. "It says here that men transmit the virus to women and to other men. So what are the health risks of HPV for men?" As they delved deeper into the FDA transcripts, Abby and Steve discovered findings that were disturbing in light of the fact that the Gardasil vaccine was now available and recommended for their preteen daughter, Ellie, but not for her twin brother, Elijah.

Steve pointed to page 33 of the FDA hearing transcript they had printed out. "Look at this! It says here that Merck actually recommended the vaccine for females between the ages of 16–29, but for girls *and* boys between the ages of 9–15. A doctor testified that two strains of the HPV infection puts men at risk for penile and anal cancer, but is also the means of transmission of HPV to women. In fact, the same two strains that cause 70 percent of cervical cancer in women— HPV 16 and 18—also cause at least 70 percent of precancerous lesions on the penis. The testimony also suggests that immunizing boys and young men would reduce the incidents of infection in the portion of the female population that might remain unvaccinated."

"I do hear what you are saying, Steve," Abby commented, "But keep reading. On page 56, it indicates that another doctor stressed that there is not enough data to support the efficacy of the vaccine for males over the age of 16. So, there is enough evidence to warrant immunizations for boys between the ages of 9–15. I wonder why the FDA did not pursue vaccinations for the boys like they did the girls? I hope this addition is just around the corner."

As Abby absorbed this information, she flashed back to numerous interactions between her, Ellie, and Dr. Smith. Ellie and countless other preteens and teenagers learn about the importance of regular gynecological exams while boys like Elijah have no established protocols, no annual exams, and no comprehensive health education to follow them throughout their lives. She said to Steve, "Ellie will start having yearly checkups about her reproductive health, but there is nothing similar for Elijah. What does this say about how our society approaches sexual and reproductive health? Where are resources for men's sexual health?

What are we communicating to young women and men about individual responsibility for relational choices and consequences?" Abby followed up, "Of course, irrespective of these broader dilemmas, we still need to make a decision about whether or not to have Ellie vaccinated with Gardasil."

Abby and Steve were mesmerized by the CNN House Calls video clip with Dr. Sanjay Gupta regarding HPV and Gardisil they found on YouTube.[4] Since their twins had introduced them to the site several weeks ago, they had secretly been playing on YouTube at night. Their fixation with streaming videos was certainly paying off now. "In thinking about the benefits of having Ellie vaccinated, Dr. Gupta's point that this vaccination can prevent 70 percent of all cases of cervical cancer is useful to consider," shared Steve.

"You know, Steve, this information also suggests the vaccination is more effective if administered at a young age, and that it can provide an added measure of protection if given before someone becomes sexually active. I suspect this is another reason why Dr. Smith is recommending the vaccination now."

As Steve absorbed this information, he stressed, "If this vaccine is as good as the Center for Disease Control[5], the National Institute of Health[6], and the FDA believe it is, then we need to seriously consider this as an option before Ellie's physical."

Abby and Steve toggled between Google and YouTube in order to investigate other benefits and risks of Gardasil and found a majority of third-party payers of healthcare are now covering the costs of Gardasil injections, including their own insurance company. "This is good news for us, given that this vaccination requires three injections that cost $120 each plus the expense of each office visit. But I wonder what it means for your brother and his daughter? He lost his insurance benefits six months ago when he lost his job," pondered Abby. After a few more clicks of the mouse, they discovered that Gardasil is now covered under a federal program available to uninsured and Medicaid eligible children under the age of 18. The vaccine is also available to many underprivileged children around the world due to Merck's outreach efforts.

"That is good, considering reports indicate that Gardasil sales have exceeded 80 million dollars. I would hope the pharmaceutical company is doing something for those who can't afford the shots," quipped Steve. "You know, we should pass this information on to my brother. Now that he is the primary caregiver for Benita, he is the one who is going to have to make these decisions. I wonder if he is even aware of these choices—their ad campaigns seem to target mothers as key decision makers, and I can't remember the last time he went to a doctor. I'm not sure how or even if he has received this information. Because cervical cancer is more prevalent among minority women, he certainly needs to be aware of all of this for Benita."

"We need to consider the risks as well," stressed Abby as she paused on the WebMD website. "Of course, no vaccine, including this one, is 100 percent effective against infection or disease, but all of the available information seems to suggest that in the case of Gardasil, there are minimal side effects." Abby and Steve identified the most commonly reported side effects of Gardasil as pain, swelling, itching, and redness at the injection site. A few girls have experienced fever, nausea, dizziness, vomiting, and fainting. "Of course, this vaccination is still very new. The clinical trials that have been done have not yet studied the long-term consequences of Gardasil. Will this impact Ellie's ability to have children later in life? No one knows the answer to that question, although I suppose we don't know anything with full certainty."

"Abby, we still haven't discussed the other major concern that parents have raised in states where Gardisil is mandated. Do you have any concerns that this vaccine will make sex seem more permissible and promote promiscuity? Does it counteract our church's message that abstinence is the healthiest choice for teenagers?"

Abby gave Steve a quizzical look. "Let's get real, Steve. The Hepatitis B vaccine does not promote drug use, does it? We would not be giving Ellie a green light for irresponsible sexual behavior! This vaccine doesn't diminish our responsibility as parents to help guide our kids to make healthy and wise choices, which begs the question of how we involve our kids in this conversation. Given that this is the first vaccine developed for a sexually transmitted infection, talking to our kids about Gardasil demands talking about sexuality."

"You know, some websites seem to indicate 12 year olds do not need to be told that the vaccination is related to a sexually transmitted disease. Instead, parents can inform them later. I don't think this is the right choice for us, though. Our kids have seen the Gardasil ads, just like you have. And, we have already opened the way for honest conversations with our kids about their sexual curiosity. I want them to be able to come to us with their concerns and questions," offered Abby. "I do like the idea of talking to both Ellie and Elijah together. The expansion of Gardasil vaccine approvals for boys seems on the horizon. Plus, sexually transmitted infections emerge from relational encounters—it's more than just women involved! I can hear Ellie's voice ringing in my ear right now, saying something like, 'how come I have to worry about it and Elijah doesn't?' She is a budding feminist."

"No kidding," smiled Steve, "She sure makes her dad proud. But, there is something else on my mind. When I think over conversations we've had about sexuality with the kids, homosexuality hasn't really been at the forefront. It makes me wonder, what if Elijah were to tell us he is gay? Shouldn't he be vaccinated too? The research indicates that anal cancer has more than doubled among gay men in the last 30 years."

"Wow . . . Steve, I've been so focused on Ellie this never even occurred to me, but you make a really good point. It seems like one incidental trip to the doctor's office has sent us into a whirlwind of choices and options. This is far more complex than I imagined."

Abby and Steve explored numerous websites that offered parental advice on how to talk with kids about HPV and Gardasil. "While I don't usually agree with religious conservatives, I agree with this one conservative columnist about one thing: this can be a good opportunity to build upon previous discussions about sex or even correct misunderstandings. Ultimately, it is still our job to help our kids understand that a vaccine is not a substitute for other responsible choices. Our kids still need to be aware of multiple consequences of unprotected sex."

"I agree, Abby. I want to include Ellie and Elijah in this conversation and decision-making process, but we had better at least think about how we are going to approach our conversation with the kids and what our 'gut' is on whether Ellie should be vaccinated."

endnotes

1. The American Cancer Society: *www.cancer.org*
2. Available: *www.fda.gov/ohrms/dockets/AC/06/minutes/2006-4222M.pdf*
3. Participating organizations included The National Institute of Health, the Center for Bioethics and Culture, the Department of Health and Human Services, the Center for Disease Control and Prevention, Wyeth Research Industry, Baylor college of Medicine, Texas Children's Hospital, and the FDA.
4. Available: *http://www.youtube.com/watch?v=k6EsQW7m168*
5. Center for Disease Control: *www.cdc.gov*
6. The National Institute for Health: *www.nih.gov*

"Heaping Hostility on Hillary"
"Isms" in the 2008 Presidential Race

*Lynn H. Turner
and Patricia A. Sullivan*

Erin put down the morning paper and turned to her daughter, who had stopped by for a visit. Today's reading reinforced her feelings that Hillary Clinton's road to the White House was going to be cut short, and she had been very involved in the campaign over the past months. She sighed, "Melinda, why does the press give Barack Obama so much love and heap such hostility on Hillary? I know you say I'm prone to rant about sexism, but in this case you see it too, right?"

Melinda shrugged, "Geez Mom . . . I just got here . . . but I'll humor you. What were you reading before I got here that made you so upset?"

"Well, I was reading another piece that reiterated how eloquent and 'presidential' Obama was in his speech about race. But really, Mel," Erin retorted, "it doesn't matter *what* I read—everything about the primaries is so biased in favor of Obama! Remember all the questions Clinton had to field about her attitudes on race? There was that *New York Times* article analyzing Clinton's stand on race that even dug out a letter she'd written to her minister when she was 13 years old about hearing Martin Luther King Jr.![1] I don't recall any questions directed to Obama about his attitudes regarding sexism. And that really bothers me. Plus, do you notice how sensitive everyone seems around race?" Erin continued. "In the primary, when Senator Joe Biden said something about Obama being 'clean' and 'articulate,' that caused a huge flap. But I recall a woman who asked John McCain early in the Republican primary 'How do we beat the bitch?' and she was talking about Hillary. McCain just laughed and answered the question without comment and none of the papers treated that as a problem. I guess it's okay to call a woman a bitch."

"Well, Mom," Melinda offered, "did you watch the *Saturday Night Live* sketch of Tina Fey when it was on T.V. or YouTube? She said it's good to be a bitch—bitches get things done!"[2]

"Oh, my goodness, Mel, you don't really believe that do you? Where have I failed you?" Erin asked. "Why is it okay to call a woman a bitch? When a conservative talk show host used Obama's middle name, Hussein, when introducing McCain, he immediately distanced himself from that comment. Why are we so afraid of that and not at all afraid to insult a woman? Remember when one columnist compared Hillary with 'the bunny boiler,' Glenn Close's character in *Fatal Attraction?* These things depress me, Melinda," Erin sighed. "And it should depress you too. There's a deep-seated hatred of women in the United States and Hillary isn't the only one paying a price for it."

"I get that this bothers you, Mom," Melinda replied, "but let's talk about something else! You're kind of overwhelming me with all this. Things have changed. After all, I'm an attorney and a mother. And besides, you know Don and I both really think Obama is great."

"I know, Mel, I know," Erin murmured. They chatted about Melinda's kids for a while and then Erin thought she would try one more time to convince Melinda to support Hillary. "Melinda, I just wish I understood why you and Don like Obama so much. Hillary is so smart and experienced, and I'd think you'd want a woman in the White House. I want your daughters to think that they could be president someday, and I know having Hillary there would be inspirational to so many young girls."

Melinda laughed, saying, "Obama is just as smart as Hillary—you don't edit the *Harvard Law Review* if you're not brilliant, Mom. To me, Obama represents a new day while Hillary is 'business as usual.' Since 1989, a Clinton or a Bush has been president—that's 20 years already—and who would want business as usual given the mess our country is in? And whether Hillary wins or not, I think my girls will know they can be anything they want in this day and age." Erin made a face and started to respond, but Mel interrupted her with a grin, saying, "I gotta run, Mom, I have to pick up the kids. We can argue about this later."

Erin wondered if her disagreement with Melinda represented a generational divide. Melinda and Don viewed Obama as a change agent who represented something "different" to remedy "difficult times." But, when Erin heard Obama's "Yes, we can" refrain, she was skeptical. First of all, it was kind of a meaningless slogan—we can do what? Where was the substance in Obama's platform? But, even if Erin overlooked that, she thought Hillary was the experienced one, the true "Yes, we can" candidate. As Erin reflected on conversations with Melinda, she wondered if she and her daughter were caught in a generation gap. Erin had read that younger voters had different perceptions of Obama than voters her age and older. And, it was the case that Hillary seemed to do better with older voters.

In an effort to understand what seemed like a generational divide, Erin read *Millennial Makeover,*[3] a book about her daughter's generation—voters from their late teens to early 30s. She had also read in the *New York Times* that the Millennials were "a generation that is in danger of being left out of the American dream—the first generation to not do as well economically as their parents."[4] Perhaps because of this, Millennials are more likely to support universal health care and see the value of government programs designed to stimulate the economy and improve job prospects.[5] The Millennials see the country as "being on the wrong track" and view Obama as their potential savior.

Additionally, if the studies of Millennials are accurate, younger voters have other reasons to embrace Obama's candidacy; his "Yes, we can" resonates with their commitment to transcend barriers based on race, gender, and sexual identity. For Melinda and Don, Hillary as a "first" or Obama as a "first" was irrelevant because those identity markers are not very important to them. Erin wondered to herself, "Would the Millennials even be willing to overlook McCain's age, since he would turn 72 before the election in November and, if elected, be the oldest first-term president we have ever had?" Although questionable comments about gender and race received press coverage, there had not been as many references to age. Erin thought this was odd considering she had read people are much more comfortable voting for a woman or an African-American for president than a man in his 70s.[6]

Obama seemed to be referring to age when he said McCain was "losing his bearings." Would comments such as Obama's be overlooked? A *Newsweek* columnist said ageism is McCain's "unseen adversary." The columnist acknowledged that people may be more comfortable acknowledging doubts grounded in age than in those based on gender or race.[7] For a clue as to how the Millennials might view McCain, Erin turned to a video posted on YouTube where two Millennials offer a litany of "McCain is older than"[8] and fill in the blank. The older than list ran the gamut from FM Radio to the Golden Gate Bridge to McDonalds® to Plutonium to Coke® in a can. He is even older than Dick Cheney. "So much for Millennials transcending 'isms' because from this video, ageism seems alive and well," Erin thought to herself.

Erin thought about how her own age played a role in her opinions. "I am 61, just about the same age as Hillary Clinton. We have similar backgrounds—both growing up in the suburbs of Chicago, and attending women's colleges on the way to graduate schools. I guess I feel like getting Hillary elected is my one chance to see someone who looks like me in the Oval Office." Erin understood that African-Americans probably felt the same way about Obama, but he was young and had plenty of time to run for president again. Erin really felt that if Clinton did not win now, there would be no woman president in her lifetime. Erin had started working on Clinton's campaign with such high hopes, and now she felt let down and deflated.

Erin left the house and stopped in at her favorite local restaurant for lunch with her friends, Tricia and Robyn. Soon they began discussing the presidential race. Tricia said, "I actually feel betrayed by the Democrats. This should have been Hillary's time."

"Agreed. You know I've noticed a disturbing trend among some of my friends. Some are planning to vote for McCain if Obama receives the Democratic nomination," Robyn responded.

"That's weird," Erin noted, "I just read in the paper this morning that women who supported Hillary were becoming more militant and tended to be hardening in their opposition to Obama. I thought that was funny because it described my mood completely. A few months ago I had said I was for Clinton, but, of course, I'd support Obama if he won the nomination. Now, I'm feeling a little differently."

"I am too," Tricia admitted. "I'm finding myself disliking Obama. He seems so smug and has such a cocky attitude."

"That's just how I feel," Erin commented. "Remember when he told Hillary during that debate that she was likable enough? Can you get cockier than that?"

"I don't think so," said Robyn.

Erin laughed, and said "It's good to talk to people who agree with me for a change. Oh, I'll vote for him when push comes to shove, but right now I feel pretty disenfranchised."

After lunch, Erin went home and called her 89-year-old mother, Joyce. Joyce lived in Illinois and Obama was her senator, but she was not supporting him. She expressed reservations about him, offering vague criticisms of his candidacy like "There is just something about him . . . I can't really buy him as President." Erin privately wondered if her mother was reticent to vote for a black man. Erin acknowledged that race was definitely an issue in the campaign because the United States has so many problems with racial division. She had read a report that many people were unwilling to disclose their "true" feelings about the prospect of an

African-American president and that some people had instigated racist incidents on Obama's campaign trail.[9] Although the Obama campaign had downplayed such incidents, his campaign workers reported encountering voters who said, "I'll never vote for a black person." Erin asked her mother, "What do you think about people not wanting to vote for a black person?"

"Well, dear," said Joyce, "maybe the country isn't ready for a black president." Erin wondered if that was code for racist attitudes. She figured it was hard to be an American and be untouched by racism and wondered if many people were unwilling to support a black candidate, but hid behind questions about Obama's youth and inexperience.

And, Erin had to admit she was bothered by Hillary's comment in an interview with *USA Today* where she claimed she had a "broader base for building a winning coalition" than Obama.[10] It was concerning to Erin that Clinton supported that assertion by saying an Associated Press article found Obama's support among hard working white Americans was weakening, and they were instead supporting Clinton. Hillary said that there was a pattern emerging; Erin hoped it was not a pattern of Hillary getting desperate and appealing to racial divides.

At the same time, Erin just could not get past her feelings that Hillary was receiving unfair treatment. As Gloria Steinem pointed out in an opinion piece for the *New York Times,* it is almost impossible to visualize a woman with Obama's credentials being taken seriously as a presidential candidate. Steinem went on to declare: "Gender is probably the most restricting force in American life, whether the question is who must be in the kitchen or who could be in the White House."[11] Erin wondered if gender was a more restricting force than race or age; it did seem like gender had held Hillary back. Hillary encountered a number of double bind situations as she presented herself during primary season. She struggled to be taken seriously in the midst of comments about her pant suits and how they were concealing "tree trunk" legs or "cankles." She remembered that even Laura Bush criticized *The Washington Post* for commenting on Hillary's cleavage. Hillary had to deal with a heckler who demanded that she "iron his shirt" at a town hall meeting.

On the eve of the New Hampshire primary, tears came to Hillary's eyes as she responded to a question about how she met day-to-day challenges in a grueling campaign. Feedback on Hillary's emotional response ranged from the laudatory to the cynical. Some commentators viewed this as a genuine moment, a glimpse of the "real Hillary." Others, however, said the moment was calculated, a sham, and one reporter even suggested Hillary was running for "Crybaby-in-Chief." Regardless of how Hillary presented herself on the campaign trail, she just could not win. Erin thought about the caricatures of Hillary from her time as first lady where she was depicted as bitch, witch, proctologist, and dominatrix. In this race for the presidency, Erin noticed that Hillary was not depicted quite so harshly, but instead the attacks on her had become more subtle and difficult to address.

On National Public Radio, Erin heard a report on witty political comebacks or "the art of the put-down."[12] The commentator suggested there was a short history of political put-downs by women because women had not been empowered politically. But the report did mention a put-down by Senator Margaret Chase Smith, the first woman elected to both the House and the Senate. In the 1940s she was asked what she would do if she woke up and found herself in the White House. She said, "I'd go to the President's wife, apologize, and leave at once." The commentator noted that such a comment would not play today. But Erin wondered if this were really true; based on responses to Hillary it did not seem that all that much had changed.

Just then, the phone rang and it was Erin's friend, Ana. Erin and Ana belonged to a book club whose members had become close friends and discussed politics. The members all supported Hillary and many had worked tirelessly for her nomination. Most of them had reservations about Obama. Erin greeted Ana by asking, "What's up?"

"I need your help," Ana replied, "I'm thinking that Hillary is about to concede and if we really want to prevent another four years of problems, we'd better get behind Obama."

"Ana, I can't believe it; but it is true things don't look good for Hillary," Erin said.

"Erin, I'm thinking that you are the one who needs to talk to our group to persuade everyone to support Barack," Ana requested.

"Why me?" Erin asked.

"Well," Ana replied, "people trust you and you are a much better speaker than I am. You also read all the papers and know about the issues."

"I'm flattered, Ana, but I just don't know if I can do that. I really still support Hillary, and I'm not sure what I would do if Obama received the Democratic nomination. I don't know how persuasive I can be when I am unsure about Obama myself."

"I understand," Ana replied. "We're all disappointed about Hillary. But in talking to some people at my gym, they sound like they are going to support McCain. It's clear to me we have to back Obama or we'll be in big trouble, so I need your help to convincing our friends."

"Well, Ana, I'll definitely think about what you've said."

"Thanks, Erin," Ana responded, "remember we have a meeting on Tuesday and there's no time to waste." As Erin hung up the phone she wondered how she could speak to her friends if she did not really believe in what she was saying, yet she knew Ana had a point.

Erin reflected on the all the conversations she had today. "What *are* my motives for supporting Hillary? I really believe Hillary is the most experienced candidate and the best person for the job, right? Or is this more about my desire to see the first woman president elected in my lifetime? Am *I* being sexist in preferring a woman? Am I thinking about the issues or the person? When it comes down to it, can Obama do for the country what Hillary could do?" She sat down with a cup of coffee and thought that this would be a long night.

endnotes

1. Leibovich, M. (2008, February 2). *Clinton's gradual education on issues of race* (online version). Retrieved September 3, 2008 from http://www.nytimes.com/2008/02/02/us/politics/02race.html?scp=6&sq=hillary%20clinton%20race%20martin%20luther%20king&st=cse

2. Fey, T. (2008, February 27). *Bitch is the new black* (video). Retrieved September 3, 2008 from http://www.youtube.com/watch?v=qHnL8mUbopw

3. Winograd, M., & Hais, M.D. (2008). *Millennial makeover: MySpace, YouTube, and the future of American politics.* Piscataway, NJ: Rutgers University Press.

4. Herbert, B. (2008, May 13). *Here come the millennials* (online version). Retrieved September 11, 2008 from http://www.nytimes.com/2008/05/13/opinion/13herbert.html?_r=1&scp=2&sq=first%20generation%20less%20well%20economically&st=cse&oref=slogin

5. Madland, D., & Logan, A. (2008, May). *The progressive generation: How young adults think about the economy* (online version). Retrieved September 11, 2008 from http://www.americanprogress.org/issues/2008/05/pdf/progressive_generation.pdf

6. Kohut, A. (2008, February 24). In November, will age matter? *New York Times.* Retrieved September 13, 2008 from http://campaignstops.blogs.nytimes.com/2008/02/24/in-november-will-age-matter/

7. "Younger than McCain." (2008, April 17). Retrieved September 13, 2008 from http://www.youtube.com/watch?v=MNYHq0WuiUo

8. Hirsch, M. (2008, January 31). McCain's unseen adversary: Ageism. *Newsweek* (online version). Retrieved September 11, 2008 from http://www.newsweek.com/id/106672?from=rss

9. Merida, K. (2008, May 13). Racist incidents give some Obama campaigners pause. *Washington Post*, p. A01. Retrieved September 13, 2008 from http:// www.washingtonpost.com/wp-dyn/content/article/2008/05/12/AR2008051203014.html

10. Kiely, K., & Lawrence, J. (2008, May 8). Clinton makes case for wide appeal. *USA Today* (online version). Retrieved September 13, 2008 from http://www.usatoday.com/news/politics/election2008/2008-05-07-clintoninterview_N.htm

11. Steinem, G. (2008, January 8). Women are never frontrunners. *New York Times* (online version). Retrieved September 12, 2008 from http://www.nytimes.com/2008/01/08/opinion/08Steinem.html

12. "Political comebacks: The art of the putdown." (2008, May 12). *Morning Edition (NPR).*

(RE)ACTING GENDER/ED REALITIES

introduction

The cases in this section illustrate people *(re)acting amidst gender/ed realities.* In our daily lives, there are times where the circumstances "are what they are," and we must find a way to operate within those circumstances. In other words, we may have to act or react to a situation that we may not like. While we may want to challenge or react to gender/ed realities, other times we have to act within these gender structures, and these cases demonstrate potential (re)actions.

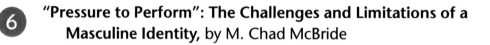

6 **"Pressure to Perform": The Challenges and Limitations of a Masculine Identity,** by M. Chad McBride

7 **"Only Skinny Girls Get the Roles": Body Image in the Dance World,** by Paige P. Edley

8 **"What Are We Supposed to Do, Mom?": A Lesson in Gender from a Bird in the Fireplace,** by Deborah S. Ballard-Reisch and Alyssa C. Ballard-Reisch

9 **"If It Makes You Uncomfortable, Get Over It": Sex Talk in the Physician-Patient Relationship,** by Jay Baglia

10 **"Is It Because I'm Female?": Challenges to Young Female Instructors in the College Classroom,** by Karla Mason Bergen

11 **"Would You Ever Make a Guy Wear Eyeliner?": External Pressures to "Do" Gender,** by M. Chad McBride

"Pressure to Perform"

The Challenges and Limitations of a Masculine Identity

6

M. Chad McBride

"Man, I'm dreading baseball practice today—I'm still worn out from yesterday."

"Well, let's plan on going out afterwards. We could definitely use the break, and it'll be great to just be able to chill."

Brett sat towards the front of the classroom listening to the conversation behind him. "That used to be me," he thought. When he came to college he made the reflective decision to not play baseball anymore, even though he had been heavily recruited by the university's coaching staff. He still loved the game, but he knew he would not play baseball professionally after college, and, to be honest, he had gotten tired of the "jock" label that loomed over his head in high school. Also, he was tired of being sore and having injuries all of the time; he always feared he was just one play away from an injury that would hurt him the rest of his life. Along with the athletics offer, he had earned an academic scholarship, so he decided to stay focused on school because he assumed that would help him more after graduation.

The problem was that the transition to college had not been as easy as he thought. It was only early October, and not only did he miss baseball more than he had thought, but he also was having a hard time figuring out how to hang with friends outside of athletics. Granted, when he was on the team he got tired of all the overly macho locker room talk that seemed to always be centered around sex, but there were a couple guys on his high school team with whom he had gotten pretty close. Now at State University, he had been hanging out with a group of guys from his residence hall, and they seemed pretty okay but they were mostly interested in drinking beer and hitting on girls; they typically went out to parties in big groups, and he really did not get to know anyone individually. He remembered back to a few weeks ago when he ran into one of the guys from his floor, Keith, on the campus quad. "Hey Keith . . . how's it going?"

"Not much . . . just tired and dreading studying for my big chemistry test," Keith replied.

"Well, we should grab some coffee after your last class. The caffeine will give you a jolt, and you could probably use some time to just chill to clear your mind. We could just hang there for a while," said Brett.

"Um . . . I . . . I think I'm busy after class . . . later," stammered Keith as he walked away.

Brett recalled thinking Keith's reaction was weird, but it was not until he ran into Greg that night that he was reminded of it. "Brett . . . um . . . did you ask Keith out on a date today?"

"What are you talking about?" Brett asked, shocked. Greg was always a little outrageous, but why would he have asked such a thing?

"Dude, Keith said you asked him out to coffee to go talk. It really creeped him out."

"He was stressed and tired. I figured getting off campus to just relax and have some coffee would help him out."

"Man, you gotta be careful. Two guys in a coffee shop . . . sounds pretty gay to me."

Brett remembered thinking Greg must be really off-base. But then again, what if Keith really had gotten the wrong idea? And did people really think that if two guys had coffee together they were gay? He had seen guys go into movies and sit a chair apart, but he never really understood what the big deal was—two guys sitting next to each other in a movie did not mean they were gay. He had gone out with guys from the baseball team, and no one ever questioned it at all. Was it just because they were athletes?

Brett was snapped back into the present as he noticed the class was stirring with everyone packing up their backpacks. It was his last class of the day, and he had promised himself that he would work out before hitting the books. The problem was that he was a little behind on the first big paper in his composition class. It was not due for three more days, but if he wanted to major in English, he wanted to make a good first impression. He decided to skip the workout and go ahead and keep working on the draft of his paper. He knew he would feel better if he made a little more headway on it.

He had originally struggled with what to write about, but his professor, Dr. Stafford, suggested choosing a topic he was interested in and already knew a little something about. He hesitated using a baseball topic, but he kept coming back to all of the performance enhancing drugs and how it had really hurt the game. Initially, he was just going to write about the steroids scandal itself and all of the congressional hearings. After reading more on the topic, he kept being pulled to the idea of the pressure to perform. It seemed like there was this increased pressure to be faster, stronger, and bigger to the point where the benchmark had become unrealistic, and it was not just for professional athletes anymore.

In doing his research, he stumbled upon a video in the library that talked about how toys had changed to reflect changes in the "ideal" body composition of men in an era of increased strength and power.[1] One point that really struck him was the comparison of the bicep measurements of "G.I. Joe" toys across time—they had more than doubled in the past 40 years. If the toys were translated to actual human measurements, they would be 26.8 inches . . . and Mark Maguire's biceps at the height of his homerun record season were only 20 inches. Of course, now it was coming out that Maguire may have been on some sort of supplements or steroids during the height of his career, so obviously these G.I. Joe figures were not realistic.

"Does this really matter, though . . . I mean, it's only toys, and will boys really even notice the arms?" Brett thought. "Do normal guys really feel pressure to look a certain way?" His thoughts turned to girls' fashion dolls and their links to body image and he recalled talking with his sister after she came home from inpatient therapy for an eating disorder. She had started treatment after their parents confronted her about her obsession with weight, even though she denied having any sort of eating disorder at the time.

"So, how are you feeling, Alissa?" Brett had asked her after she came home.

"I'm doing okay. It was a tough process, and I had to really be honest with myself about some of my obsessions," Alissa said.

"What were you obsessed about? Food?"

"No, and that's why I never thought I had an eating disorder. I was obsessed with working out—everything you always hear is how important it is to work out and have an active lifestyle. I had never heard of exercise bulimia, but now I know it was what I was suffering from."

"So what's the difference then between exercise bulimia and working out on a regular basis?" Brett asked.

"Well, like other eating disorders, exercise bulimia has to do with control, but it can turn into something that controls your life. People with the disorder compulsively exercise to the point where they miss work or parties, work out while sick, and become seriously depressed when they can't work out. It's all part of the same body image issues that afflict other bulimics and anorexics," explained Alissa.

"But you've always been very fit and had a good body. Where did the body image issues come from?" Brett asked.

"Well, I can't give any one source. You know how I always obsessed over my magazines, and the introduction of size 00 clothing didn't help any. I mean, every advertisement has people with more than six-pack abs, but they're all airbrushed. It's just totally unrealistic."

Brett thought that if his own sister had body image issues from mediated images, surely boys could think the same things when seeing the bulging muscles of toys and sports stars. He decided to take a short break from the paper to let all of these ideas stew. He picked up his latest issue of *Men's Health* and started perusing some of the pages. He had gotten a subscription because he wanted to explore new workouts since he was not working out with the team anymore. What seemed like a good idea at the time now sometimes overwhelmed him. Every month there was a different set of workouts, which he could kind of handle because he liked changing up his workouts. The harder part was that every month there was a litany of "eat this . . . not that" and different supplement or vitamin suggestions. He could not keep up with what were the good things, and what they were good for. Reading it, he often felt overwhelmed by all the suggestions.

"Wait a minute, how is this any different than what Alissa was talking about? I know I don't obsess over this magazine in the same way, but I can see how it could happen," thought Brett. As he flipped through the pages, he started paying more attention to the pictures. "All of these guys are totally ripped. I've always considered myself to be fit, if not athletic, and my body has never come close to looking like this. I can't imagine how much more I would have needed to work out when I was on the team to be this cut. I mean, the title of this magazine has health in the title. If this is healthy, I've never been 'healthy' a day in my life."

He remembered all of the injuries he got on the field, but his coach always yelled at them, "Be a man! Play through the pain!" He certainly did not miss putting his body through that, but now, instead of the pressure for his body to be faster and stronger, it seemed like as a non-athlete he had pressure for his body to look a certain way. "I know I'm not nearly as fit as I used to be, but it's hard to fit workouts into my schedule. I guess that was another good thing about being on the team . . . I never had to work out on my own or worry about what I was eating . . . we were always running our butts off."

Just when Brett was thinking about how to incorporate all of these ideas into his paper, Greg and Scott walked in his room and chided: "Hey dude, get ready . . . we're going out tonight."

Brett replied, "I just don't think I can. I have this English paper I'm working on. . . ."

"Is it due tomorrow?" asked Scott.

"No, but I want to . . ."

"Man, don't be such a nerd. You can do it tomorrow—there's gonna be hot chicks at this party. Don't you want to get some?" interrupted Greg.

"Okay . . . I guess I'll go. Give me half an hour to get ready." Brett really was not interested in picking up a woman, but the party might be fun . . . and he *had* been missing male friendships earlier in the day. After getting out of the shower, he reached for a pair of jeans and noticed he had to suck in more than usual to put them on. He had heard about the 15 pounds people put on in their first year of college, but he always thought it was an exaggeration. He had not gained that much, but he was obviously a little bigger than when he had shown up on campus. "Maybe I do need to quit skipping my workouts and start eating a little better . . . it's just that those chicken fingers sometimes look like the only edible option at the cafeteria," thought Brett.

A bit later, he hopped in Greg's car as they sped off to the house party. When they got there, people were standing around everywhere drinking out of the usual red plastic cups. He looked around for options, but all he found was the beer keg and some sort of reddish punch in the trash can. Just then, he saw Greg and Scott walking back up to him.

"Hey Brett—here's a cup we got for ya," said Scott.

"Oh, I think I'm fine . . . I've got an early class in the morning, and I'm just not feeling like drinking tonight," said Brett.

"Dude, I thought I already told you to lighten up. You don't want people to think you're some kind of dork. Come on . . . be a man," chastised Greg.

Brett reluctantly took the cup and started mingling around the party. He recognized a few people from campus, but there were a lot of new faces as well. He walked over to a group of people from his History of Western Civilization course.

"Hey Brett, how's it hanging?" said one of the guys he recognized. "This is Meg and Sasha, they're both sophomores."

Brett stood chatting with his classmates and the two women for quite a while. Before he knew it, he had reached the bottom of his cup and decided to go ahead and get a refill. After he excused himself from the group, he ran back into Greg and Scott.

"Dude, who's that hot blonde babe you were talking to?" asked Scott.

"Oh, that's Meg . . . she's friends with some people in class," replied Brett.

"You've got to be hittin' some of that tonight," said Greg as he slapped Brett on the back. Brett did think Meg was attractive and seemed pretty cool, but he was not really interested in hooking up with someone for just a one night stand.

"Nah—she seems like a nice girl. I'm sure I'll run into her again . . . then maybe I can get her number," replied Brett.

"God, get it together. If you don't make a move tonight, she'll probably think you're gay or something. I saw the way she was looking at you . . . she totally wants you. Put on your stud hat, and go back over there," said Greg.

Brett went back to the group but never made any moves for Meg. She seemed really awesome, but he was more of a relationship type of guy and liked to take things slow. On the car ride home, Greg kept giving him crap about not making a move. He played it off, but it started to really bother him. "Why is it that a guy who hooks up randomly is such a stud? If Alissa did the same thing, she would be labeled a slut or whore," thought Brett. "It seems like such a double standard. For me to be seen as a 'real man' I have to play the field, but we have all of these negative words to describe women who sleep around. Who do we think all of these studs are sleeping with?" He never really hooked up like that in high school, but baseball players had a reputation on campus as being popular with the girls. Personally, he had never really lived up to the stereotype, but he realized now that as a baseball player people probably just assumed he hooked up with girls and never really questioned him about it. The theme of pressure on men from his paper popped back into his head—was this just another way men were pressured to perform? His *Men's Health* did always have several articles about getting laid.

When he was lying in bed that night, he kept going back to the interaction between the teammates in his class earlier that day. In some ways life seemed so much easier then. His masculinity was never questioned when he was out with another guy. Was it because everyone knew he was a baseball player? Now it seemed like if he wanted to study, skip a party, not drink, or not hit on a girl, he was questioned. Back then, he was never accused of being gay or a nerd—now he felt this pressure to fit into this little box of what it meant to be a man. He was not any different than he was in high school . . . maybe as a baseball player, he had this masculine façade that protected him from getting all of these questions and judgment. "How can I still be seen as a masculine guy and do what I like to do without playing baseball?" To top it all off he was starting to get a little self-conscious of his belly. He knew he could start working out more on his own, but if he were on the team it would be like killing two birds with one stone—his masculinity would not be questioned and he would have built-in workouts. He had gotten out of baseball so he would not feel the pressure to be bigger and faster like the professionals, but he was feeling just as much pressure now—just in different ways.

"Maybe I need to just suck it up and go talk to the coach about trying to walk on the team. I know he said the door was open as long as it was before pre-season practice, and I'm pretty sure that's starting here soon. I know it would take up a lot of time, but in some ways it seems as if life would be easier. I wouldn't have to explain myself as much or do things I didn't want to do," thought Brett. He rolled over in his bed. If he wanted to go out for the team, he would need to talk to the coach tomorrow.

endnote

1. Katz, J. (1999). *Tough guise: Violence, media and the crisis in masculinity* [video-recording]. Northhampton, MA: Media Education Foundation.

"Only Skinny Girls Get the Roles"

Body Image in the Dance World

Paige P. Edley

After her early evening jazz class, Kara approached her dorm suite that she shared with three other girls and imagined a familiar scene: Jenna and Callie would be sprawled on the living room floor of their suite watching TV and flipping through magazines, and Jill would probably not be home from the gym yet. Sure enough, as she was opening the door she heard the TV, and when a trailer came on for a new movie with the newest tall/slender Hollywood "It" girl, Callie whined in typical form, "Ooh, I wish I could be that skinny! She's so beautiful!"

Jenna rolled her eyes and grumbled as she held up her fashion magazine to show a page to Callie and then flashed the magazine at Kara. "Speaking of skinny, look! Every woman on this page is emaciated. I would have to work out five hours a day and eat only carrots and celery to look like that. They must starve themselves."

Kara walked in, threw her backpack and dance bag in the corner and collapsed on the sofa, sinking her tired body into its soft cushions. "Well, I certainly am not one to starve myself, and after dancing all day long I'm famished! What do we have to eat?"

"It's so refreshing to hear a dancer want food!" said Callie. "Before you got home, we were talking about Jill. We're worried about her. As you can see, she's not home yet, and we're just hoping she's having dinner or something and isn't at the gym. You both dance all day long as dance majors, but then she still goes to the gym in between classes to run on the treadmill for an hour. She's really fit, but *so, so* skinny. . . ."

Jenna interjected, "When we went to the gym together yesterday, I saw her jump on the scale three times during her workout—totally obsessive—and when we met for lunch on Wednesday, all she did was push her salad around her plate with her fork."

"I'm worried, too," Kara confessed. "But I'm hoping it will pass. She has an audition on Monday, and she's obsessing about her weight."

"That explains it! It's the audition. The media have ingrained in us that we have to be a size 0 or we are worthless to society . . . only the skinny girls get the roles," Callie exclaimed.

Kara looked down at the floor and sighed, "Yeah, well it's not only the media. Our teacher adds to the pressure by telling us to cover up our bellies unless we want to work on them. She made us wear booty shorts and crop tops for our midterm last week. It was humiliating. I was bloated and she pointed out every flaw; she even found things to criticize about Jill's body. She said it was to prepare us for auditions so we'll be ready to audition in skimpy outfits."

"She had no right to make you feel bad about yourself," Jenna comforted. "You can kick your leg up over your head while smiling that beautiful smile of yours. Forget what the teacher said . . . look at these women in the Dove Real Beauty campaign in my magazine. These are what non-dancer bodies look like, Kara. The standards you and Jill are striving for are so intense!"

Callie agreed. "One of my professors studies how media organizations influence our body image. She has done research on dance and theatre majors on campus and how they feel about their bodies—especially in this Hollywood-influenced campus with so many young women trying to break into the entertainment industry here in Los Angeles."

"I swear half the campus is anorexic or something—it's just not normal," Jenna said.

"My professor said in class that her research showed 22 percent of the dancers had exhibited characteristics of an eating disorder. Would you agree with those stats, Kara?"

"Yeah, she actually interviewed me for the study. Personally, I try to keep it in perspective so I can be healthy, but I think the pressure—and Professor Chasse's criticism—has gotten to Jill. A lot of us are worried about her and a couple other girls too. One senior started a support group to bring awareness of eating disorders to the dance majors, and she serves as a liaison to Student Psych Services. We should probably get Jill to talk to her," Kara decided.

"Well, if your teacher is reinforcing these unrealistic norms of the media by nit-picking your bodies, it seems like there is a bigger problem here," prodded Jenna. "Other girls who we aren't roomies with are probably acting just like Jill. I think you should talk to your dance teacher, Kara . . . for the health of you, Jill, and who knows how many other dancers."

Kara sat in silence. She agreed with her friends, and knew that until the mid-term Jill had not been quite so obsessive about her weight. "But couldn't I just get Jill the help she needs and not deal with Professor Chasse? That might impact my future here in more ways than one if I am seen as a whistleblower or rebel in the dance department. Yet, she really is abusing students, even though she says it's for 'our own good'," she thought.

"Girls, I see your point. But for tonight, let's think about how to approach Jill and let me sleep on what to do about our teacher."

"What Are We Supposed to Do, Mom?"

A Lesson in Gender from a Bird in the Fireplace

Deborah S. Ballard-Reisch
and Alyssa C. Ballard-Reisch

KEY TERMS

- ◆ socialization
- ◆ motherhood
- ◆ empowerment
- ◆ gendered roles

"You can do anything you set your mind to." "Your abilities are limited only by your capacity to be creative." And later "don't let the limitations someone tries to impose on you determine who you are" were all messages Kate tried to instill in both her son and daughter as they were growing up. As a single parent, Kate was careful to train both her children in cooking, cleaning, and yard work. Sometimes Robert did get more difficult chores initially, not because he was a boy, but because he was almost five years older than Aly. Kate was careful to train Aly in those chores and shift responsibilities in an age-appropriate manner.

When Aly was 14 and about to start high school, Kate moved her to a new town so she could accept an exciting job offer. Because Robert was a sophomore in college, he stayed behind in their prior home and it fell to Kate and Aly to undertake the exciting adventure of setting up a new home in a new city together. When Aly expressed typical teenage concerns about moving to a new place, Kate reassured her, "Aly, just give it until Christmas . . . by then you will make new friends and it will feel like home." Fortunately, Kate was right. By Christmas, Aly had a strong group of friends who came to the house regularly to hang out or for pizza and movie nights or to play pool.

This new city was more politically and culturally conservative than their prior home, so Kate continually reminded herself, "I have to find ways to help Aly to stay strong and confident in her power and abilities and know that girls can do anything." She knew the cultural messages Aly was receiving now challenged the empowering messages Kate had tried to create earlier in life, and she tried to circumvent the messages about appropriate behavior for girls in this new area.

One spring Saturday morning, Kate sat on the living room couch reading the newspaper as Aly slept in. Suddenly, a small bird insinuated itself into the living room fireplace, its entrance heralded by scratching, cheeping, and a plop that disturbed the placement of the logs. The bird's arrival startled Kate, and she leapt off the couch. She rushed to the fireplace and looked in. There, panting at the bottom of the pit was a small sparrow. Kate noticed that she had not yet turned off the pilot light to the fireplace and feared that the bird would suffocate. She opened the cover to the fireplace controls and tried to turn off the pilot. She could not move the knob—either she was doing something wrong or she was not doing it with enough force. She rushed into Aly's room, shaking her daughter awake. "Hey, come help me, a bird is stuck in our living room fireplace."

Aly's first response was "humpf, I'm sleeping Mom. Are you dreaming? The fireplace is closed in. We'll get it later."

Kate responded, "No, no, I was sitting on the couch, and it just plopped down. We have to get it out! The pilot light is on and I'm afraid it will suffocate! Just come see."

Aly got up and looked in the fireplace. The little bird was getting excited now, fluttering to the top of the fireplace and back down, bumping into the glass front. "I'm afraid it will hurt itself," Kate said "or worse—I couldn't turn off the pilot light—it could be gassed to death."

Aly was now getting riled up as well. "Well, Mom, I've never done this—what are we supposed to do?"

Kate caught herself before blurting out her initial thoughts to "just call Casey's dad next door." She always wanted Aly to feel empowered to figure things out on her own and not resort to relying on a man when it came to tasks like this. They could probably search for the manual and eventually figure it out, but if they took the time to do that the bird may already be lost. Or they could call Casey's dad and have him run over, which might increase the chances of saving the bird. But would that send the wrong message to Aly that a man should come to the rescue? Kate knew she did not have much time to make a decision.

"If It Makes You Uncomfortable, Get Over It"

Sex Talk in the Physician-Patient Relationship

Jay Baglia

Dr. Jennifer Margolis, a family medicine practitioner, had just returned from a few days of vacation to celebrate her 30th birthday and was catching up on the electronic medical records (EMRs) of her patients. In particular, she wanted to see the results for Tom, a 58-year-old diabetic who she had admitted to the hospital for a couple of days in order to complete some fairly routine diagnostic tests. After getting past her initial guilt in not being there some of the days he was hospitalized—after all, no primary care physician (PCP) can work 24 hours a day, 7 days a week—she turned her attention to the content of Tom's EMR.

She noticed that on the days when she was not at the hospital, Tom had been seen on daily rounds by Dr. Aaron Grasse, who was one of her faculty colleagues. She was taken aback to see that Tom had been prescribed Viagra®, the popular treatment for erectile dysfunction, upon his release from the hospital. She knew she would see Aaron later that day at a faculty meeting, so she made a mental note to ask him about it.

"Hey Aaron, do you remember my patient Tom that you saw on rounds this weekend? What motivated your prescribing Viagra for him, anyway?" asked Jenn.

Aaron replied, "During my visit, Tom talked about how in 'intimate' moments with his wife, he was having trouble achieving an erection. So I prescribed him the magic little blue pills to help that along, that's all."

"I've been treating Tom for five years," Jenn began, "He's never indicated to me that he wanted or needed Viagra."

"He was probably embarrassed," offered Aaron.

"But I'm his doctor," countered Jenn, "I talk to him about lots of things—it makes me wonder if he is keeping anything else from me."

Their conversation was overheard by several other physicians at the meeting. Noting Jennifer's obvious misgivings, Dr. Marcus Cairo attempted to intervene. "Don't take it personally, Jenn. He probably asked Aaron because he's more comfortable asking another man," Marcus reasoned.

"That's ridiculous. It shouldn't matter. I'm his doctor. We have an excellent relationship." Jenn was clearly upset by this line of argument. After a brief pause, she added, "He's even said on more than one occasion that I remind him of his daughter."

"Well there you go," replied Marcus. "How comfortable could a man be, asking his daughter for help with his sexual problems?"

"That's not what I was implying," countered Jenn. "We have a strong relationship. It's exactly the kind of relationship that we try to model for our residents."

"But Jenn," pleaded Marcus. "This involves sex. It is what it is."

As Jenn seemed to acquiesce to her colleagues' rationalizations, another physician, Dr. Cheryl Bennett, chimed in on the conversation. "Jenn, have you ever asked Tom about his sexual activity? I mean, have questions about sex or sexual behavior ever become a regular part of your history-taking?"

"Not with Tom," Jenn offered.

"But with your other patients?" Cheryl asked.

"Some of my other patients," Jenn replied honestly.

"Do you think that if you included questions about sexual activity as a standard component of your patient visits that they might be more comfortable talking to you about sexual problems?" Cheryl inquired.

Marcus weighed in. "I think you're all making too big a deal out of this. At the end of the day, the patient asked Aaron for the Viagra and Aaron prescribed it. Jenn's informed because it is part of the electronic medical record—as long as she knows Tom is taking it, everyone who needs to be informed is informed."

Cheryl pursued the conversation further. "But Marcus, isn't Jenn, as Tom's doctor, entitled to a conversation with him. I mean, why does he even need Viagra?

Is it because of other medication side effects? Is he depressed? Is he happy in his relationship? More importantly, now that he has a prescription, and Jenn knows this, has he taken it and is it working? Shouldn't they be able to discuss this?"

Aaron, who had been silent through much of the dialogue, posed the question more directly: "Jenn, do you even want to have this conversation with Tom?"

At home that evening, Jenn asked her husband about his relationship with his physician. "Jeff, you have a female PCP. Is there anything you wouldn't want to talk to her about?"

Jeff considered the question briefly and then replied, "I guess I might be a little uncomfortable if I had to talk about sex."

"Really?!" Jenn was incredulous. "Why do you think that is?"

After pondering for a minute, Jeff said, "For me, the reason would have to do with boundaries. I trust my physician with just about everything. I guess what enables me to have the relationship I do with my doctor is that it doesn't include such private matters."

A few weeks later, at the next faculty meeting, Cheryl sat next to Jenn to share some timely news: there was a workshop slated for later in the month about some of the issues of patient interaction Jenn was concerned about. "They even have jargon for it," Cheryl began, as she circulated the lecture announcement. "It is called 'discordance' and 'concordance.' The speaker has published several essays in the *Journal of Sexual Medicine.* These terms are used in research to describe the gender makeup in the physician-patient relationship. If the physician and patient are of the opposite sex, they are discordant and if they are of the same sex they are referred to as concordant. Jenn, you and your patient are gender discordant."

Along with dozens of residents, Jenn and most of the faculty attended that lecture on discordance and concordance and its impacts on the physician-patient relationship. While Jenn found the subject interesting, the results were far from conclusive. She learned, for instance, that physicians in a variety of specialties reported and perceived discomfort when interviewing opposite gender patients as well as patients who were very young or very old.[1] The presenter, Dr. Will Bastian, a professor of communication, theorized that "This discomfort may be partially attributable to the fact that both female and male physicians in primary care see far fewer patients of the opposite sex while in residency, and in general, female patients tend to outnumber male patients, making up on average two-thirds of the patient population."[2,3]

To make matters even less clear, Dr. Bastian reported that "while one study related to patient satisfaction reported low rates of satisfaction when patients were examined by younger physicians of the opposite sex,[4] another study found the greatest satisfaction between male patients of female physicians."[5]

The physicians then broke into small groups to apply the research findings to their own experiences. These small group discussions revealed that patients tended to speak longer with female physicians than male physicians; disclosed more information during the family and psychosocial history; and made more overall positive statements to female physicians.[6]

Once the groups reconvened, Dr. Bastian further muddied the waters, noting that, "All this information I have presented so far is less relevant when the focus turns to sex, sexuality, and particularly, examinations related to the anus, breasts, and genitals." He continued, "In one study, significant differences between male and female residents were apparent regarding their comfort in managing gender-specific health-care topics involving physical examination of parts of the body that are generally revealed to the opposite sex only in intimate situations." When he asked for feedback from the audience, the residents expressed some discomfort while examining the opposite sex but conceded that this may be culturally and/or educationally based.

Jenn thought again about her patient Tom and whispered to Cheryl, "We *both* may have been hesitant to open up the conversation about sex due to our age difference."

At the next faculty meeting following the workshop, Marcus entered with a smirky grin. "I've got something to tell you guys." Before launching into his story, he quickly recounted the conversation about Tom, Aaron, and Viagra, as well as the topic of the workshop for the benefit of those faculty members who needed additional context.

"So my patient Kody comes in today. He's 40 years old, black, in pretty good physical condition. No major problems. He's married and he has two young children. I explain to him that now is a good time to have his prostate checked. When a man reaches the age of 40, I tell him, a 'digital' prostate exam is recommended. Kody agreed that a digital screening 'sounds like a good idea,' and so I start putting on the rubber glove, asking him to remove his pants."

Several member of Marcus' audience now begin to anticipate where this story is going. "So Kody has this weird look on his face," Marcus continues, "and it's pretty obvious that he and I didn't understand each other. It turns out that Kody thought a digital exam referred to something computerized. He didn't realize the exam would entail me inserting a gloved, lubricated finger into his rectum."

After an awkward pause, Jenn glanced around the room, exhaled, and exclaimed, "See, it's not just me!"

"Obviously it's not just you," said Aaron. "Otherwise there wouldn't be dozens of research articles about this."

Marcus' story was countered by female physicians whose male patients did not tell them about sexually transmitted diseases, and male pediatricians whose female patients changed doctors upon reaching puberty. What all these stories confirmed was that, despite the best intentions of the physician, the patient cannot always neatly separate the professional context of medical care from what might be the sexual tension that may arise whenever two people, whether of opposite or same sex, gay or straight, discuss matters related to what is often considered private.

At a Continuing Medical Education (CME) event later that month, Jenn listened to her colleague, Dr. Holly Pfenning, a family physician, explain the need "To be cognizant that female patients are much more accustomed to being 'probed' than male patients as they routinely undergo pap smears once they become sexually active." Holly contrasted this to men, who, with regard to genital health, "rarely see a doctor unless something's wrong." She reasoned that men have external genitalia, so they can often "feel" when something is wrong, as in the case of a testicular node, or "see" an abnormality, as with the visible signs of an STD.

This led a gynecologist in the audience to speak up, arguing that a conversation about sexual health is the responsibility of every primary care physician since patients may not otherwise offer the information. She asserted, "I can empathize that for those of you who work in family medicine or internal medicine, the challenge of talking about sex with your patients—particularly if they are of the opposite sex and if they are older—can be daunting. But the bottom line is, if it makes you uncomfortable, get over it."

Jenn sat in a bit of a stunned silence . . . given her recent situation with Tom, the generalized comment struck a personal chord with her. Did she need to "get over it?" In the short term, should she bring up the Viagra issue with Tom and ask why he was not comfortable talking with her? But more importantly, with her male patients in general, what should she build into the interview about sexual health and sexual history? How could she make the male patients more comfortable talking about these issues with her? Jenn had some decisions to make before seeing her male patients.

endnotes

1. Burd, I., Nevadunsky, N., & Bachmann, G. (2006). Impact of physician gender on sexual history taking in a multispecialty practice. *The Journal of Sexual Medicine, 3,* 194–200.
2. Paluska, S., & D'Amico, F. (2000). The comfort of family practice residents with health care of patients of the opposite gender. *Family Medicine, 32,* 612–617.
3. Fennema, K. (1990). Sex of physician: Patients preferences and stereotypes. *Journal of Family Practice, 30,* 441–446.
4. Hall, J., Irish, J., Roter, D., Ehrlich, C., & Miller, L. (1994). Satisfaction, gender, and communication in medical visits. *Medical Care, 32,* 1216–1231.
5. Schmittdiel, J., Grumbach, K., Selby, J. V., & Quesenberry, C. P. (2000). Effect of physician and patient gender concordance on patient satisfaction and preventive care practices. *Journal of General Internal Medicine, 15,* 761–769.
6. Hall, J., & Roter, D. (2002). Do patients talk differently to male and female physicians? A meta-analytic review. *Patient Education and Counseling, 48,* 217–224.

"Is It Because I'm Female?"

Challenges to Young Female Instructors in the College Classroom

Karla Mason Bergen

"How'd your class go?" Kathy asked Liz as they met in the hallway outside the graduate teaching assistant (G.T.A.) offices.

"I'm not sure I'm cut out for this," Liz confessed. "I'm just totally frustrated with these students. Do you think we were ever so disrespectful to *our* professors as undergrads?"

"What do you mean, 'disrespectful?'" probed Kathy as she unlocked the door to their shared office.

Liz followed her in and flopped down in her chair by the window. "I'm tired of being addressed by 'hey' in student emails and by my first name in class. I'm tired of all the side conversations in class while I'm talking. And most of all, I'm tired of students arguing quiz answers in class when they are clearly wrong."

"Yeah, I know what you mean," said Kathy. "It's different being on the other side of the desk. My first semester as a G.T.A. was a freaking disaster. I had a group of girls who sat in the back of the room and whispered to each other the whole class period. When I tried to call them out and make them stop, they just got worse. I finally had to enlist the help of my advisor and the department chair. I was so shell-shocked that I just T.A.'d for Dr. B the next semester . . . I didn't feel like I could handle a class on my own."

"Well, you must have learned something since then," Liz observed. "You're teaching your own stand-alone Interpersonal class this semester. What's the secret?"

"Actually, Dr. Baker had me do an independent study that semester I was her T.A.—a literature review on classroom management and gender. One of the things I found out was that young women instructors typically have more difficulty with classroom management than young male instructors. Can you believe that?"

"Do I find it hard to believe the students give us a harder time because we're female? Not at all! It's pretty hard to take when I hear students calling Micah down the hall 'Dr. Smith' while they call me 'Liz.' He's no closer to his Ph.D. than I am!" Liz snorted.

"Yeah, and that's not just your experience—that sort of experience is backed up by research studies," Kathy affirmed. "Researchers have found even *young* male G.T.A.s get more respect from students than young female G.T.A.s if you judge by how they address the teacher. But one other thing I've found is that experienced female professors actually report they seem to get more respect and fewer challenges from students as they teach longer and get older."

"That's depressing," said Liz. "So what can we do other than wait to get older or dye our hair gray?"

"Well, one thing that really helped me was talking to Dr. B about how she handled situations in the classroom and reading about how other GTA's and professors had learned classroom management skills," Kathy offered. "I remember a handout I found in the Teaching and Learning Center here on campus, 'Tips for New G.T.A.s'—all of the tips started with the word 'communicate.' I'm sure I still have it around here somewhere." Kathy rifled through the notebooks on her shelf. "Okay, here it is—'Communicate clear expectations'—that's mostly to do with laying your policies out on the syllabus at the beginning of the year. That's probably the most important one. . . . hmm . . . okay, 'Communicate the image of a competent professional,' 'Communicate with a cool head,' 'Communicate to maximize the positive outcome for both you and the student.' Here, I'll let you read this for yourself. Maybe there's something in there that will help you."

"Communicate clear expectations? I thought that's what I did on my syllabus and in class on the first day," thought Liz. "I wonder if any of our male colleagues are having any of these classroom management problems? The research must be right—how am I supposed to deal with it if it is a gender issue? I never thought I'd need a clause about talking or being rude in class. How can I go about making my expectations about classroom behavior more clear at this point in the semester? Or do I just try to tough it out and keep notes on what to include on the syllabus next semester?"

"Would You Ever Make a Guy Wear Eyeliner?"

External Pressures to "Do" Gender

M. Chad McBride

April reviewed the agenda for her first speech team captain meeting of the year. On it was a proposal for new guidelines about "speech team dress and appearance." She assumed the proposal stemmed from last year's national tournament where there was a big discussion surrounding the ways the team members should present themselves to be more successful as individuals and a team. She thought, "I am dreading this meeting! I know where this conversation is going . . . and I really don't want to deal . . ."

April still remembered the "situation" at nationals. After her teammate Laura advanced to semifinals, their coach Conrad matter-of-factly suggested, "Laura, before the round, make sure to put on a little concealer and eyeliner and change into your suit that has a skirt."

Since Laura typically wore no makeup and rarely wore skirts, she had come to April to express her frustration. "April, I can't believe he wants me to put on makeup. Where is this coming from?"

April did not really like wearing makeup much either and had talked with both Conrad and the assistant coach, Monique, about the issue in the past. One morning, at a previous tournament, Monique had told her, "April, you're looking pretty tired from staying up late rehearsing last night—adding a little concealer will just make you appear more rested and competent for rounds."

Across situations and individuals, Monique and Conrad's argument was consistent: "Speech is a type of public performance, and so whether we like it or not, appearance comes into play when the judging takes place. Just as actors wear stage makeup to make their eyes stand out in theatre, we want you to have the same effect—eye contact is really important."

April shared this argument with Laura. "Conrad has lots of experience with national speech tournaments and has seen that competitors who appear more put together tend to do better in close rounds. He just wants us to be more successful."

"Yeah, but how many of the guys on the team have been told to put on eyeliner before their rounds? And certainly none have been expected to wear skirts," Laura retorted. Since April was not sure how to respond, she decided just to bring everyone together.

In that informal meeting, Laura told Monique and Conrad she felt there was a double standard that men did not have to wear makeup for their final rounds. "Well, I've suggested to a few guys to put some concealer on their eyes and their zits before rounds before," Monique said.

"Yeah, but would you ever make a guy wear eyeliner?" Laura asked.

Conrad then gave his perspective. "Laura, this may sound harsh, but like it or not, there are some double standards when it comes to women in some contexts. I know the players on the women's basketball team have to shave their legs, but obviously the men don't. And I know the women on the softball team are encouraged to wear their hair longer to fight off the stereotype that they're lesbians. Perception matters, especially when you're being judged. We're not telling you how you need to look any other day." In the end, Laura ended up putting on some makeup, but April remembered Laura had been very upset about "giving in" after the fact.

After recalling the events that had led to the "speaker dress and appearance" proposal on the agenda, April turned her attention to how she felt about it, and what she would say at the meeting. She suspected the proposal would add makeup to the list of suggested appearance requirements for competitors. On one hand, she saw its merits; within the speech community culture, it was expected that women wear makeup and project a particular appearance to please the judges, and since the competitive success of the team impacts Conrad's job with the university, she could see where he was coming from. On the other hand, speech is still a student activity, and this guideline perpetuates stereotypical expectations of appearance for women in society. So is it okay to perpetuate double standard expectations for females if it is within a particular culture that values it for competitive purposes? Is it okay to have "mandates" or even suggestions for how women should look? If makeup really makes a woman more competitive, is it not still her choice how competitive she wants to be? April looked at the clock and knew she had to head over to the meeting soon. She was not sure how much of a stand she should take on the proposal. Maybe she would be moved one way or the other in the moment.

(RE)CREATING GENDER/ED REALITIES

introduction

The cases in this section profile individuals who are *(re)creating gender/ed realities* in light of having a major life change (i.e., adopting, stay-at-home parenting, disability, sex reassignment, etc.). These cases highlight the power we have to create (and recreate) gendered identities for ourselves and others—illustrating that identity is never completely fixed or static.

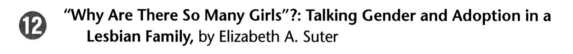

12 "Why Are There So Many Girls"?: Talking Gender and Adoption in a Lesbian Family, by Elizabeth A. Suter

13 "When Do I Get a Break?": Unexpected Emotions for a Stay-at-Home Dad, by Caryn E. Medved

14 "Do We Need to Make It Look Good?": Form, Function, and Femininity for Women with Disabilities, by Laura L. Ellingson

15 "It Can't Be Domestic Violence . . . We're Just Dating": Keia's Story, by Loreen N. Olson and Sacheen K. Mobley

16 "Can a Man Be a Feminist?": Moving from Dominance to Alliance, by M. Chad McBride

17 "Starting Life with a Clean Slate": Kylie's New Job, by Sherianne Shuler

"Why Are There So Many Girls"?

Talking Gender and Adoption in a Lesbian Family

Elizabeth A. Suter

- ◆ race-ethnicity and gender
- ◆ sexism
- ◆ patriarchy
- ◆ identity formation
- ◆ patronymy
- ◆ self-esteem
- ◆ mothering

A few years ago, Susan and Kay, a Caucasian lesbian couple, decided to build their family via transracial, international adoption. Susan and Kay adopted Meilyn from China when she had just turned one. Just after they adopted Meilyn, they were told by their adoption agent, Barb, about Colorado Heritage Camps, Inc., an organization that annually runs ten camps focusing on adoptees and adoptive families with heritages ranging from African/Caribbean to Russian/Eastern European to Chinese.[1] While Meilyn was now seven, this was only the third year they had made it off the waiting list of Colorado Chinese Heritage Camp (CCHC) and into the actual camp, held at the YMCA of the Rockies Snow Mountain Ranch facility in Fraser, Colorado.

Resting in the family cabin one morning after staying up too late playing Mahjongg, Kay somewhat mindlessly looked at the camp literature that was on the coffee table along with a listing of services and amenities. "As a nonprofit post-adoption advocate and resource organization, Colorado Chinese Heritage Camp is a pioneer, emerging in 1997 at a time when only a handful of culture camps existed for families with children adopted from China. Today, CCHC is a large, vibrant camp that annually accommodates 200 plus attendees. The importance of CCHC is underscored by the growth in U.S. Chinese adoptions. During the last decade and a half, the number of children adopted from the People's Republic of China has increased more than any other country, and China has ranked as the top country of origin for U.S. international adoptions since 2000. Workshops for children are at the heart of camp, offering children opportunities to explore and learn about their birth culture and their identity. Simultaneously, camp provides workshops for adults ranging from explorations in Chinese culture to discussions of how to grapple with issues of racism, grief, and loss as they parent their child. Nestled in the Rocky Mountains, Snow Mountain Ranch provides a serene setting for families to get away from their everyday lives."

She remembered being told by Barb that at camp, "Parents and kids are literally unplugged. Your cell phone reception will be spotty and there is limited, if any, internet connectivity. Instead of watching TV with Meilyn, you will have the chance for campfire talks and playing board games and cards." Barb emphasized how this fosters connection between camp attendees and opens up both a space for and a willingness among adoptive parents and adoptees to explore aspects of identity and culture.

Reminiscing about Barb made Kay think about Meilyn's toddler years and the lifebook that she had created for her. A lifebook preserves information and photos about a child's life before he or she was adopted. Once the lifebook was completed, Susan and Kay read it to Meilyn as a way to practice telling their daughter her adoption story as well as a way to introduce adoption language and make it seem part of normal conversation. When Meilyn was four, it felt like she became keenly interested in the book overnight. She would often get it down from the shelf herself, engrossed in the pictures of her life in China before coming to the United States. She peppered her mothers with questions about details in the pictures. Around five, her questions shifted to how and to whom she was born, demonstrating her development and newfound awareness of some of the larger issues addressed in the book.

While Meilyn expressed a mild curiosity about her birth father, her curiosity about her birth mother was seemingly insatiable. Taking cues from books she had read about talking to children about adoption and advice from an adult adoptee friend, Kay never shied away from these conversations. Rather, she used them as opportunities to allow Meilyn to explore her thoughts and feelings, inviting Meilyn to draw pictures or to create names of what she envisioned her birth mother might look like or be called. Although common wisdom in past generations led parents to shy away from such conversations, Kay was not threatened by yet another mother in Meilyn's life. Indeed, Meilyn already had two mothers at home.

Susan and Kay were impressed. The lifebook seemed to be fulfilling its promises to develop a positive sense of self-esteem and a positive ethnic identity in the adopted child. Meilyn was proud of being Chinese and anxiously awaited the family's annual trek to the mountains to both celebrate and learn more about her heritage. Meilyn had also easily integrated adoption language into her vocabulary—for instance, deftly able to differentiate between her birth mother and her adoptive mothers in conversation. This task was perhaps more difficult for Meilyn than for many children because she had two mothers and needed to negotiate different mother names for Susan and Kay. Meilyn was taught to call Susan "Mama Susan" and to call Kay simply "Mom." Since 2007, Meilyn, on her own volition, had begun dropping the "Mama Susan" and had starting calling both of her mothers "Mom."

Kay's thoughts were cut off by a sweaty and very excited Meilyn rushing in from outside. "Hey Mom, do we have any Gatorade® left? Jade and GiGi and I are playing and we are really thirsty."

Kay smiled, responding, "Plenty of Gatorade in the fridge, kiddo, help yourself."

Meilyn started to head toward the kitchen, but stopped halfway and in her typical off-hand way asked, "And, oh Mom, have you ever noticed how it's like *all* girls at camp? Where are all the boys? Why *are* there so many girls?"

Trying to keep her surprise in check, Kay heard herself saying in a rather calm sounding voice, "That is a great question, Meilyn. Let's sit down and talk about it when we have more time. Go enjoy Jade and GiGi."

That seemed to satisfy Meilyn for now. She returned to the kitchen and was out the door waving Gatorade saying, "Love you, Mom."

After Meilyn ran outside, Kay sighed. "With all the conversations the lifebook has already initiated, why did Meilyn's question catch me so off-guard?" she wondered. Still puzzled, Kay realized her time would be better spent sorting through what she already knew, what she needed to know, and how to fill in the gaps *fast* so she could provide Meilyn an honest, yet developmentally appropriate, answer.

Kay found herself thankful she had woken up in time for yesterday's adult workshop on Chinese culture. Who knew the information would prove helpful only a day later? The workshop had been led by Professor Johnson, an adoptive mother of a daughter from China and a Professor of Asian Studies and Politics at Hampshire College. Professor Johnson presented information about China's one-child population control policy and its cultural gender bias toward boys. Kay learned that after World War II, China experienced a population explosion. In an attempt to curb its increasing population, China introduced the one-child population control policy in 1979. Yet, it did so seemingly without consideration of the cultural gender bias toward boys.

Professor Johnson explained how China's gender bias derives in part from the Chinese belief that only males can pass on the family name, what she said other scholars have termed patronymy. Johnson's written materials included a quotation that stuck out to Kay, "Male children are often preferred over female children because males can give birth to future generations in name, while females cannot."[2] Professor Johnson was quick to point out that "patronymy is far from unique to China and instead can be seen in many cultures, including the United States. But, patronymy might be particularly ingrained in China, as opposed to other countries, due to Chinese persons' intense reverence for ancestors and their belief in continuing the ancestral line." Johnson also explained that in addition to the ideology of patronymy, the gender bias toward boys may be further exacerbated by daughters' transfer of familial obligations to their husband's family upon marriage, leaving the son to stay and take care of his parents. Johnson talked about how she hoped her own aptly titled book, *Wanting a Daughter, Needing a Son*[3] would help inform Westerners about the combined pressures created by population control policies and the gender bias towards males that lead many Chinese birth mothers to relinquish their daughters for adoption in hopes of providing their girls a better future.

Just then, Susan swung open the cabin door, singing out, "I'm home."

Kay rushed to give Susan a hug, "Wow, am I ever glad to see you."

Kissing Kay, Susan responded, "Now that makes coming home worth it. Love you too. But why the puzzled face?"

"Sit down Suzikins," Kay said as she plunked herself down on the sofa. "I need your advice."

Susan snuggled in. "I'm all yours. What's up, my Kay?"

Kay recapped her thoughts about the lifebook and how Meilyn's question had burst her bubble, ending with, "You know, for all the work we have done talking with Meilyn about her adoption, I am at a loss for why I was so caught off-guard by her question."

"We *have* been diligent about creating space for Meilyn to talk about her adoption," Susan responded, sitting up. "But, think about it. We have always followed Meilyn's lead. Since the gendered aspects of her adoption had yet to dawn on her, we have remained remarkably silent on those issues. I have to say I have been wondering when the other shoe was gonna drop, but I didn't really want to try and explain it all to a seven year old. So, I am just as much to blame as you are. I wonder if Anne and Nora (Jade and GiGi's moms) are also just hanging out in their cabin. Want me to run across and see?"

Leaning in, Kay whispered, "This is why I love you. Thanks."

Susan walked the short distance to their longtime friends' cabin. The four women had been friends since college. Anne and Nora had adopted Jade in 1998 and then GiGi in 2000. So, when Susan and Kay made the decision to adopt Meilyn, Anne and Nora were right there to help them through the process. The four had moved from just friends to best friends to feeling like family. Arriving at the cabin, Susan knocked. Nora answered, "Hey woman, come in. You're looking a bit frazzled. What's up?"

"We need you and Anne. Meilyn just popped the gender question," Susan replied.

Calling out to Anne to slip on her shoes, Nora said, "Well, it had to come sooner or later." Grabbing a bottle of wine, Nora added, "We might need this."

Kay smiled as the three blew in, with Anne announcing, "Gender trouble in paradise, Kay?" Anne was both amused and informed by how Kay had deftly encouraged and then facilitated discussions with Meilyn about aspects of her adoption, such as loss and grief, that would have left other parents tongue-tied. Anne continued, "You know I always manage to say the wrong thing at all times to both Jade and GiGi. You would think that I might get it right at least on my second try with GiGi. But, oh no. So, I'm happy to share my mistakes so you can do it right, Kay."

After scrounging up four chipped coffee mugs, Nora began distributing the wine. Handing Anne a mug, she said, "Oh, Anne, the *worst* one happened after you came back from Professor's Johnson's workshop last year."

Anne groaned, "You have to hear this one. So, I am all stoked after the workshop, excited by my new-found knowledge. I come back to the cabin to find Jade and GiGi quietly playing together. I called them to attention and gave them a lecture on Chinese population control laws and cultural gender bias towards boys. I realized midway through that it was totally developmentally inappropriate, but for some reason, I kept on going. Finally, I stopped and asked the girls what they thought about it all. So, after a very long pause, Jade slowly said, 'No wonder they let you adopt us. Two girls. We aren't worth much to the Chinese.' To make it even worse, I then got totally judgmental, telling Jade, 'No. No. Don't feel *that* way. You just aren't thinking about it correctly.' The more I dismissed Jade and GiGi's feelings, the more their feelings tumbled out. GiGi had recently been teased at school at first for having two mommies and then it switched to how they 'throw away baby girls in China.' So, GiGi interjected, 'I guess what Bobby said is right after all, they do throw away girls in China. I never ever want to go back to China—even just for a visit.'

"But, rather than encouraging either of my girls to talk about their feelings, I was quick to reject their feelings and tell them how they had it all wrong. Finally, they figured out that mom was not really gonna listen to them. So, as quick as the feelings had poured out, they drained dry. What is really sad is that since then, when I bring up the subject, they both say, 'I don't want to talk about it.' They are not giving me a second chance on this one, which is so frustrating. If anyone can get it right, Kay, it is you."

Kay smiled slightly, "Thanks for the vote of confidence." She was interrupted by Meilyn, Jade, and GiGi bursting in, complaining that they were starving. The moms laughed and both couples decided it was time to get their families' dinners started.

After Anne and Nora left, Susan brought Meilyn to the kitchen to be her assistant, leaving Kay alone with her thoughts. Kay found herself wondering, "How am I gonna answer Meilyn's question? I couldn't be more grateful for the information I have gained from camp and to Anne and Nora for sharing their experiences. But, I still don't feel like I know what to say. I think I have a better idea of what *not* to say. There are so many issues to consider. Meilyn has had a big day, and I am emotionally exhausted, so I think it will be better to bring this up over Rice Krispies in the morning. Who knows, maybe a good night's rest is all I need to figure out what to say."

endnotes

1. This chapter is based on the author's scholarship on adoptive and lesbian families as well as her experiences as an adoptive mother of a daughter from China. While Colorado Heritage Camps, Inc. is real, the people and the events are fictive.
2. Lebell, S. (1988). *Naming ourselves, naming our children.* Freedom, CA: The Crossing Press.
3. Johnson, K. A. (2004). *Wanting a daughter, needing a son: Abandonment, adoption, and orphanage care in China.* St. Paul, MN: Yeong & Yeong Book Company.

"When Do I Get a Break?"

Unexpected Emotions for a Stay-at-Home Dad

Caryn E. Medved

Painting and sculpting had always been Nelson's passion, and then after college this passion turned into his career. As an artist, Nelson always worked nontraditional hours and took time off between projects. Sales of his artwork brought in spurts of income, while his wife Denise's salary at the bank provided for their modest but comfortable life. So when they had their first child two years ago, it made sense for him to be Gabby's caregiver in her early years. What Nelson did not expect was how tough life could be as an at-home dad.

"Okay, Denise," he had said on the phone around noon, "You're lucky. Tonight I'm going to make some mushroom risotto, fresh asparagus, and some luscious tiramisu. You've been working too hard!" Denise had already told Nelson she would not be home until late that Friday night. Long meetings had kept her at the office until after 8 P.M. all week, and Nelson was feeling a little lonely spending his days with Gabby while having limited adult contact.

"That sounds wonderful! I'll stop and get a bottle of wine on the way home. Has Gabby had her nap yet today? I'll be home by 8:30. What a week," Denise replied with a weary voice.

"I'm putting her down as soon as I'm done cleaning up the lunch dishes— I'm hoping she'll sleep long enough that she can stay awake until you get home tonight. With all your meetings you've barely seen her, so hopefully we'll *both* see you later!" Nelson closed.

But Nelson's best laid plans began unraveling when he went to the pantry and there was no risotto. "Okay Gabby, let's get in the stroller. We're taking a walk to the grocery store!" As they walked the three blocks to Balducci's Gourmet Market, Nelson saw a group of mothers playing with their children in the park. He often longed for adult contact, but the one time he stopped over to play with Gabby in the park, he got the looks of quizzical admiration, as if people were thinking, "How cute! A father with his daughter in the middle of the day . . . I wonder where her mommy is . . ." He just found it too hard to have to explain to them why he was staying home. He had tried before, but people could not understand that he actually loved his role as primary caregiver.

In Balducci's, he stared at the shelf and then he asked the sales clerk, "Hey, do you have any risotto? I don't see it on the shelf where it usually is."

"Nope—all out," he responded without stopping.

"Ahhh, Gabby, we'll have to go with this flavored rice junk, but it'll do. Let's go." Later that evening, the dinner situation spiraled for the worse. While Gabby sat in her high chair with some apple slices, the phone rang. The local librarian who commissioned a picture for the lobby said she did not like Nelson's painting. Already upset from the phone call, Nelson realized he forgot the asparagus, and when he opened the box of rice, he accidentally spilled it on the floor. "I'm about to give up—when do I get a break?" he shouted to no one in particular.

Just then, Denise walked in the door with a bottle of wine. "Hey, I got off work early. Isn't it great that we get some extra time as a family?"

"Well isn't that just great," he snapped. To his surprise, in that moment he found himself resenting Denise and her time away from home every day (and recently, every night). "I just managed to drop our entire dinner on the dirty floor. This is ridiculous. Do stay-at-home moms have days like this?" Nelson exclaimed. He tried to sound like he was joking, but he really was feeling upset . . . so much that he was actually choking back some tears.

"It's okay, thanks for trying," Denise said as she took off her coat and put down the wine.

"That's easy for you to say, you haven't been shopping and cooking all day while watching the baby, only to have your meal spill all over the floor!" Nelson complained with an apron on and an empty box of rice dinner in his hand. They tensely stared at each other for a minute. Nelson shook his head and thought to himself, "Why am I so upset? I feel silly! I'm not much of an artist, and I can't even make dinner. How can I find a way to balance my time with Gabby and also have regular adult contact so that I am happy in my life and in my marriage?"

"Do We Need to Make It Look Good?"

Form, Function, and Femininity for Women with Disabilities

Laura L. Ellingson

KEY TERMS

- ◆ ability
- ◆ physical appearance
- ◆ femininity
- ◆ identity formation

"This way," said the cafe hostess, leading through the maze of tables filled nearly to capacity with a boisterous lunch crowd. Meredith crutched awkwardly through the narrow spaces, still learning to balance following the surgery that had amputated her right leg several inches above the knee. She watched with interest as her companion Judy walked smoothly and without hesitation. They settled at a table against the wall and perused the menu.

A week earlier, Judy had introduced herself to Meredith in the waiting room of the dentist they shared. She remembered those first words: "I hate to be presumptuous, but my name's Judy, and I have been an amputee for more than 20 years. When I saw you come in, you still seemed pretty slow and deliberate on your crutches. If you don't mind my asking, was your amputation recent?" Far from being offended, Meredith had been excited to meet another woman amputee—the vast majority of amputees are men—and had eagerly accepted Judith's invitation to meet for lunch today.

"So," said Judy, a smile lighting her carefully made-up face. "How has it been going?"

"Well," Meredith hedged, not wanting to sound whiny. "Pretty good. The phantom pain is still a problem, but my limb has finally lost enough of the post-surgery swelling that I can start the fittings for a prosthetic leg, which is encouraging."

69

"I remember how difficult it was for me at first," replied Judy. The two women talked about recovering from the devastating loss of a limb. For Judith it had been the result of a car accident when she was 22 years old. For Meredith, the amputation was the latest in a 20-year-long series of surgeries following a child-hood diagnosis of cancer. Meredith felt enormously comforted by Judy's empathetic responses. Judy continued, "And the new prostheses look so realistic, no one even notices I am wearing one." Meredith looked down in surprise as Judy kicked her leg out. Beneath the cuff of her crisp blue capri pants, Judy's prosthesis did indeed look remarkably like her other leg, even sporting an elegant pair of high heeled sandals.

"I thought you couldn't wear heels with a prosthesis?" asked Meredith hesitantly.

"Oh yes! This is my high-heeled leg," Judy explained. "I have several different legs—some for wearing heels, one for flat shoes, one for going to the beach. Of course the beach one is pretty ugly—I wouldn't wear that one anywhere else, you know—but it's great for getting in the water. And the rest of my legs look just as realistic as can be."

"Your insurance paid for a special prosthesis just for wearing high heels?"

"Oh no, I paid for it myself. I've collected different legs over the years. But insurance will pay for the cosmetic foam covers that go over the prosthesis. They understand that women don't like having all those metal and plastic parts showing," Judy said.

Meredith stared at Judy in surprise. Still coping with the painful transition to being an amputee, it had never occurred to her that she would want to invest thousands of dollars in a prosthesis just for wearing high heels or that she would want to cover up the working parts of her prosthesis. She looked down at her cotton khaki shorts and her white cross-trainer style sneaker which contrasted sharply with Judy's smart outfit and understated gold jewelry. Meredith never wore make-up and seldom remembered to add earrings or a necklace to her outfits. More often than not, she skipped styling her hair and pulled it back into a convenient ponytail. She was much more worried about how she would ever manage to ride a bicycle or go for a walk in the park with a prosthesis than she was about how the prosthesis would look to others.

Listening to Judy, she began to worry that she had been too focused on function and not enough on appearance. Maybe others were staring at her not because she was different, but because she was ugly? Was being an amputee inherently unfeminine? Should she cover up her leg in public and try to "pass" as a person without a disability?

"It Can't Be Domestic Violence . . . We're Just Dating"

Keia's Story

Loreen N. Olson and Sacheen K. Mobley

KEY TERMS

- gendered abuse/violence (emotional and physical)
- relational power
- self-esteem
- dating/courtship
- masculinity

Keia was your typical college freshman. Raised in a small, bedroom community in Florida, she was the youngest of four children and the only girl. Both her parents and her brothers reinforced her position as the "baby girl" of the family. She felt very loved and cherished. She had a boyfriend in high school but decided she needed a fresh start when she went to college so they decided to break up the summer after their high school graduations. Now, she found herself straining her neck to see the top of the 12-story cement building in front of her—her new home, the newest co-ed dorm on campus.

Surrounded by a sea of unfamiliar faces all moving into the dorms at once, Keia was undaunted, for she was too excited about this new opportunity at independence. "Hurry up, Mom! I want to see my room before my roommates get here," Keia yelled down the stairs to her mother, who lugged a suitcase behind her. As she walked down the hall, Keia marveled at how many people were crammed into the halls . . . playing catch, moving in, saying "hi" to old friends, and making new acquaintances. "This is perfect!" Keia exclaimed, clutching her mother's hand and pulling her into the suite that was to be her home for the next year.

As Keia's father and brothers brought in the rest of her things, she walked up and down the hall checking out other residents. "Hey, my name is Keia, what's yours?" she asked a girl moving in next door.

"I'm Candace, and this is my brother Kevin." Candace indicated the boy bringing the box through the door. Keia was a little speechless. Kevin was very cute. She held out her hand to him as he put the box down.

"Hi, are you a student here as well?" Kevin asked, shaking Keia's hand and smiling at her.

"I am. I'm a freshman, and you?" Keia responded to his handshake and his smile with a smile of her own. "I'm a junior over in the business school. Looks like you and Candy are going to be neighbors."

Keia heard her Dad calling her name and moved out the door past Kevin. "Yeah, I gotta go, but it was nice to meet you both." "Same here," Candy said as she moved down the hall towards a stack of boxes. Keia drifted back to her family, wondering if she would run into Kevin again.

The first few weeks of school flew by for Keia. The busyness of attending freshman orientation, picking classes, making new friends, and joining organizations occupied every waking moment Keia had. One highlight was how consistently she ran into Kevin in the residence halls. Kevin often complimented Keia about how hot she looked and seemed to really be interested in her thoughts and ideas. They frequently talked until the early morning hours about music, politics, etc. They seemed to enjoy the same things—even the philosophy course first year students were all required to take! Talking on the phone one evening, Keia told her best friend, "it's like we're one person. We see the world so similarly, it's freaky!" Keia waited patiently for Kevin to take their relationship to the next level.

One day the wait was finally over. As Keia passed Candy's suite, Kevin shouted out, "Hey you!"

"Hey," she said back and paused in the doorway to chat.

"I've been meaning to ask you something," Kevin said as he moved in close to her. Keia felt as if her heart would leap out of her chest. Then he said, "Would you be interested in going to the homecoming dance with me this year? It's still a few weeks away, so you'd have plenty of time to find a sexy dress to wear."

"Ahhhh . . . . . ummmm . . . . . mmmhhh . . . . let's see . . . . oh, yea, *yes,* of course. I'd love to," Keia stuttered, trying to hide her excitement.

Homecoming, and the weeks following, was so magical that Keia could not believe it was her life. Kevin really seemed to know how to treat a woman—he read her like a book. He was a real romantic and often left sweet little notes on her stack of books or in her day planner. The night he said I love you will live with Keia forever. She knew the relationship was moving fast, but everything felt so right. One day when they ran into each other unexpectedly outside of the student union, Kevin bent down to kiss her. The spark between them from that kiss seemed to seal the deal on a great relationship. "You look very pretty today. What is the occasion?" Kevin asked, holding her tight.

"I went to an informational meeting for Alpha Kappa Alpha sorority," Keia responded.

"Oh," Kevin said frowning "are you thinking of pledging a sorority next year?"

Keia was a little taken aback by the frown, "Well, the women in my family traditionally pledge AKA so I wanted to at least go and listen to what they had to say. I am going to the Delta Sigma Theta informational tomorrow and to the Sigma Gamma Rho informational on Friday. It is turning into a busy week!"

"Hmm, have you really thought about what joining a sorority will do for you?" Kevin asked.

"Well, yes, I have," Keia responded. "There are many years of history and pride for my family as well as life-long connections and friendships. I think those are good reasons to think about it. Why? Do you disagree?"

"Well, no, but it is a big time and money commitment. Not to mention joining one severely limits chances for an outside social life. You might just want to make sure you have given it some more critical thought."

Keia looked at Kevin and wondered if he was right. She had spoken with her parents about this decision, and they were very supportive. However, they were obviously biased because they had both pledged into a fraternity and sorority and assumed their children would as well. All of her brothers were part of a fraternity as well as many cousins and aunts and uncles. Being a part of the Black Pan Hellenic Council seemed like an obvious choice for Keia, but now she had her doubts. "Well, I have some time to think about it since we cannot pledge before our sophomore year. I am sure I will spend more time talking to my mom and dad about this before I make a final decision," Keia said moving down the hall towards her suite.

Kevin retorted, "Just remember, Keia, college is about what *you* want to do; not what your parents think you should do. You're an adult and can make your own decisions. Talk to you later." As Keia and Kevin parted company, she pondered her new role as an adult away from her parents and family.

October turned into November and Keia and Kevin's love seemed to deepen. He was so sweet. He often called or IM'd several times during the day to see how Keia was and what she was doing. She even liked how he would show up at clubs when she was out with her girlfriends. He told her he did this because he missed her. Keia liked that. It made her feel special and protected. Before she knew it, it was time to go home for Thanksgiving break. Keia needed to pack, so Kevin decided to come over and help her out. "Really, you didn't have to come. I'm just throwing some clothes in a bag. And my books—geez, I have so much to do that I'm almost sad to go home, but I miss my family so much." Keia pulled clothes out of the closet as she chatted to Kevin and Candy. "Are you all going home?"

"I am," Candy said, "Kevin has decided to stay here and go home for Christmas."

"Yeah, I have a project due right after break and, besides, I don't need to run home as much as some people," Kevin responded.

Candy threw a pillow at him. "Whatever, I miss mom and dad, so I am going home. I hear my phone, back in a flash." Candy bolted out the door and down the hall.

Keia was quiet as she finished packing her bag, thinking about the fight she and Kevin had the night before. Kevin rolled off the bed and walked over to her, putting his hand on her shoulder, "Are you okay?"

Keia shied away from him, "My shoulder still hurts a little from last night." Kevin moved over to the suite door and closed it, "I am sorry Keia. I did not mean to push you. I just got a little jealous about the idea of you running into your old boyfriend while you were back home. I love and care about you a lot. I would never hurt you. I didn't really think I pushed you so hard that you would bounce off the wall like that. You just seemed excited to see him, and I thought maybe you might be missing him."

Keia walked over and sat on the bed with her hands clasped in front of her, "I am not used to people getting angry like that. In my family, we don't hit."

Kevin sat down next to her and took her hands in his, "I didn't hit you. I pushed you, and I am sorry. I will never hit you, but you made me really angry. I just lost control. It won't happen again, I promise." Keia looked at Kevin and believed him. Her parents taught her that everyone makes a mistake, and she was sure Kevin was sincere. She felt better about their relationship and went home for break, thinking about their special bond.

Fall semester ended with Keia completing her first semester as a college freshman with a 3.8 GPA. Her parents were proud of her for making the Dean's list. Keia was also proud but confused. Her relationship with Kevin seemed, on the surface, to be going well but appearances were deceiving. She was beginning to feel more controlled by Kevin but, at the same time, she felt very protected and cared for. He was more critical than anyone else in her life, but his suggestions were not all bad. He did not like all her clothes but was willing to pay for clothes he thought she looked good in. And, it turned out that he was right—she did look better now that her hair was a little longer. He could be mean sometimes but he was also a lot of fun, and he apologized whenever he knew he hurt her.

While Keia was aware that she was sporting an assortment of bruises under her clothes from arguments with Kevin, she considered those arguments and not abuse. She would talk herself out of worrying about the situation: "Kevin and I just have arguments. Besides, we're just dating—abuse is something that happens between a husband and a wife, right? And, to be honest, it isn't all his fault. I get just as upset with him and yell back, too." She thought it was good of him to never hit her in a place that would show and he always said he was sorry after a big argument, promising never to get that angry again. She spent part of her semester working in the Women's Studies department so she had a working knowledge of what abuse "looked like," and she felt she was not in that kind of relationship. She and Kevin had a lot of fun, worked well together, had a loving relationship—her parents even liked him. He was kind and considerate to her and seemed genuinely to want what was best for her.

"Hey Keia!" Candy crossed the grass towards her. "How are you? I have not seen you in a while. How did your semester end?"

"Very well, I made the Dean's list, which was my goal," Keia responded.

"That's cool! All those late night study sessions with my brother must be doing something for you!" Candy smiled at Keia knowingly, "He really likes you. You are, practically, all he talks about. Are you really coming to visit over break?"

"Yes. I am going home for most of it but will be at your place for New Year's. I am excited to meet the rest of the family."

"Hey, did you fall down or something? That is a nasty looking bruise on your arm?" Candy asked as she reached for Keia's arm.

"Yes, I tripped coming up the stairs the other day. I can be a little klutzy when I am tired" Keia responded, tugging her sleeves down.

"Oh, well, be careful, we would not want anything to happen to you. My mom is so excited to meet you. Kevin never brings girls home so she thinks you must be pretty special. Gotta run, see you later" and she walked away, leaving Keia alone with her thoughts. Though she felt troubled by some aspects of her relationship, Keia also felt very special to be Kevin's girlfriend, and talking to Candy reinforced that attitude.

By Spring Break, Keia was feeling the pressure of college life and a tumultuous relationship. College was still fun and exciting but the workload was heavier this semester. She decided to apply for the joint pre-M.D./J.D. Program offered next fall, and making sure she had the prerequisites was keeping her very busy. In fact, to Kevin's dismay, she was much too busy for a social life. "I never see you. Every time I call, you are in the library, heading to the library, or going to a study group. Maybe you should rethink this decision since you obviously don't have enough time for everything you are committed to," Kevin said as he lounged in the doorway of Keia's bedroom, watching her get dressed for their date. "Why are you wearing that anyway? I don't like you in black; it makes your skin look ashy. Wear the white outfit instead and take your hair down." Keia changed clothes and pulled the clip out of her hair.

Kevin moved towards her to play with her hair, and Keia shied away from his touch. Her cheek was still bruised from the last time he came near her face. "Why are you pulling away from me? I said I was sorry. Besides, the bruise is already fading and you can cover it with makeup." As Keia walked to the bathroom to fix her makeup, Kevin walked up behind her and pulled her close in an embrace, "You know that I would never intentionally hurt you. I just got a little upset. I don't think you need to pledge a sorority. You don't need people telling you what to do and what to think. I understand you want to please your parents but I am your man, you should be asking yourself what *we* need, not what *you* need."

Keia felt guilty for not discussing her decision with Kevin, but she knew he would not approve. She tried to be a good girlfriend, but it seemed that everything she did set him off these days. He was very stressed and was not doing as well in school as she was and that was causing many arguments. He wanted so much of her time now and she was so busy. It all felt like it was spinning out of control. "Kevin, I really want to join Delta Sigma Theta. I have the grades, and I like the girls. I think it will be good for my career and my self-esteem," Keia said leaning into his embrace.

Kevin tightened his arms, "Are you saying that I am not good for your self-esteem?"

Keia tensed, hearing the subtle change in his voice, "No, I think I need some outside support for my studies, and I want to follow in my mom's footsteps, even if it is a different sorority."

Kevin tightened his embrace more. "What about me Keia? I have another year of school, and then I am trying for graduate school. How are you going to be here for me and be a part of that as well? Why do you think they will even take you? You're smart but you can be lazy without someone staying on top of you."

Keia pulled away from Kevin, "You know, *I* made the Dean's list and am on course to do it again, so I think I am pretty motivated." Keia moved towards the bathroom door.

"So now you think you're better than me?" Before she could respond, Kevin pushed Keia into the door and spun her around. She went down to her knees, gasping for air from the blow to the stomach. As Keia began to cry, Kevin realized what he had done and picked her up from the floor holding her in his arms. "I am so sorry Keia. I love you. I am just stressed right now. I would never hurt you. But, boy, you really push my buttons when you do things that don't put us first. But, I really am sorry . . . please forgive me." Kevin continued to profess apologies for his behavior as he helped Keia get to the bathroom to clean up for their night out on the town.

As she applied her makeup, Keia couldn't help but think to herself, "Do I really deserve to be treated like this? I know I can be pushy; should I stay with Kevin and learn how to be a better girlfriend to him? No one else, including Candy, seems to think his behavior is problematic. Maybe an occasional push isn't such a bad thing. We all lose our temper. Besides, Kevin's really a good person. And, I love the way he loves me. It makes me feel secure and wanted. But, I have to be honest, look at me. He just hit me in the gut. Is this really okay?" Closing her eyes and taking a deep breath, Keia whispers, "Please, please help me decide if I should just leave or try and work things out."

"Can a Man Be a Feminist?"

Moving from Dominance to Alliance

M. Chad McBride

Ben sat as his desk while he was prepping for his Gender Communication class later that afternoon. As he was looking over his notes, an email popped up from Damon, a student in his gender course. Stopping what he was doing, he clicked on the email, which read, "Dr. Irving: I was reading the description of feminism, and I got to thinking, Can a man be a feminist? I always thought feminism was a negative word, but based on this, I think I might even consider myself a feminist. Just thought I'd ask before we got in class and everyone was listening. See you in a few hours, Damon." Ben appreciated the question because he had often pondered this issue himself—but he had never come to a definitive conclusion.

Later, Ben joined two of his colleagues, Morgan and Leigh, for lunch in the conference room. "So today in Gender, we're talking about feminism and how for a lot of people it's the new 'f-word.' I just got an email from a male student who asked if it was possible for men to be feminists. Leigh, I know we've talked about it before, but I'm still not sold on the idea."

"Ben, you *teach* gender communication, you do gender research, you're a planner for Stop Intimate Violence Week, and didn't you just get elected to the women and gender studies board? How can you *not* be considered a feminist?" questioned Morgan.

"Well, yeah. And of course I teach gender from a feminist perspective that critiques societal structures instead of teaching about sex differences," said Ben.

"And for most of your life, you were raised with two sisters by a single mother—you have literally been surrounded by women. I know you want equal rights for them and can appreciate the patriarchal system that makes it harder for them," said Leigh.

"No, you're right. I do feel like I partially understand what it's like to be a woman since I was raised mostly by and around women. And certainly I'm an advocate for female causes and issues, but I can never understand fully what it's like to be a woman in our society. I mean, when I left night class last night, I never had to think about, 'Is there someone behind me?' or 'Is everything lit up enough for me to feel safe?' I've heard women talk about how they think about the possibility of being attacked anytime they walk outside in public at night by themselves," Ben said. "I can honestly say I've never really considered that in the moment. I mean, I just walk out to my car. I can't imagine having to consider that possibility on a regular basis."

"Ben, just the fact that you can even consider that experience from a woman's point of view means you think about things from a different perspective," suggested Leigh.

"Yeah, but I'm still a man. That example is pretty cut and dried, but what about more complex ones? Aren't I reinforcing a patriarchal system if, as a man, I suggest I know what's best for women?" Ben wondered.

"But Ben, there's a whole history of people within the dominant group advocating for the oppressed group," added Morgan. "Look at all of the white people that marched along with blacks in the civil rights movement. And I'm a straight woman, but I still think I can speak out on LGBT[1] (lesbian-gay-bisexual-transgender) issues."

Leigh pressed Ben further: "And isn't your discussion also going to address the typical negative connotations of feminists as man-hating or lesbian fascists? I mean, I'm an open feminist, but I changed my name when I got married and I obviously wear makeup and care about fashion and jewelry. How can we ever change the negative stereotype of 'feminist' if all types of feminists, including men, don't stand up and speak out?"

"I guess you're right. Maybe I'm erring too much on trying not to reinforce a patronizing structure for women." But Ben still was not sold. He never wanted to come across as a "know-it-all" man, but he certainly supported female causes. He pondered how he would frame the discussion and attempt to answer Damon's question. Can a man just be a supporter of feminism? Or can a man truly label himself as a feminist?

endnote

1. LGBT (also GLBT): either of these expressions are acronyms for individuals who are lesbian, gay, bisexual, or transgender/transsexual. The acronym differs across organizations; for example, the Human Rights Campaign (HRC) utilizes GLBT while the Gay, Lesbian and Straight Education Network (GLSEN) utilizes LGBT.

"Starting Life with a Clean Slate"

Kylie's New Job

Sherianne Shuler

KEY TERMS

- transgender
- gender reassignment
- identity formation
- gender transition
- discrimination

Kylie stared at the computer screen, blinking back tears as she read and reread the e-mail. It was April of her senior year, and she had already secured her dream job with a Fortune 500 company in Chicago. On June 1, movers would arrive in her small college town in the Midwest and move her belongings to a tiny apartment in Chicago, where she was scheduled to start an intensive management training program. She had interviewed with the representatives on campus and been flown out for an exhausting but exciting two days of onsite interviews and accepted their job offer without hesitation a few days later. She could not wait to be starting life with a clean slate.

Shortly after arriving on campus as Kyle four years ago, she began undergoing the process of gender transition. Even as a small boy, Kyle felt deep down that he was meant to be a girl. With the support of the LGBT (lesbian-gay-bisexual-transgender)[1] student group and its faculty advisor, Kyle began to embrace a feminine identity in his freshman year. With the assistance of the residence life staff, she moved into a co-ed dorm and lived as a woman and also started taking hormones. Kyle's parents had a hard time with it at first, but they were doing their best to be accepting and loving towards their child who now wanted to be their daughter. During the summer between junior and senior year, Kylie had gender-reassignment surgeries, and three months ago, she completed the legal paperwork necessary to become a female.

While she had supportive friends at her small liberal arts college, she longed to go somewhere new where she could just pass as a female and not be seen as a curiosity. Even though she was not the first transgendered student at her college, she was the first to complete the gender reassignment process while in school. The plan to move to Chicago seemed her ticket to normalcy, until today. Her new supervisor's e-mail was asking for a copy of her transcript, which still identifies her as Kyle. When she applied for the position, Kylie used her female name, and her letters of recommendation and resume all discussed her as female. When she reports for work, she will use her (new) female driver's license and social security card to fill out the company paperwork. Until now, there was no mention of needing to provide a transcript, which is one of the things she had been worried about. This company is the type she had dreamed about working for, but they were not exactly known as progressive about LGBT issues. Since she had already completed her transition, she had hoped that would not matter. The training she would get there would be worth keeping her mouth shut for a few years, and many people had told her that if she did well in her first few years there she could pretty much write her own ticket and go anywhere after that.

She grabbed her cell phone and immediately dialed her boyfriend, Juan to tell him about her dilemma. "What do I do?" she whined, "Do I tell them the truth and risk being fired or at best being seen as a freak? Last time I talked to them, the registrar's office said that they would not change the name on my transcript. And we all know that Father Janko isn't the most comfortable with trans issues, so I don't think I will get much help from the Dean's office. What are the chances that they will agree to delete the references to Kyle and use Kylie?" Juan listened for a minute, but could not really offer any advice right then. He was already getting annoyed looks from the other people waiting in line with him at the DMV, and he could not exactly talk about this topic in public. After they hung up, Kylie turned back to her computer and reread the closing lines of the e-mail:

"Sorry I didn't mention this before, Kylie, but we need the transcript ASAP. The company will pay whatever is necessary to put a rush on it. Let me know the soonest you think it can arrive. Looking forward to having you join us! Warmly, Joanna Smith."

She would have to figure something out, and quickly. Kylie sighed and reached for her cell phone.

endnote

1. LGBT (also GLBT): either of these expressions are acronyms for individuals who are lesbian, gay, bisexual, or transgender/transsexual. The acronym differs across organizations; for example, the *Human Rights Campaign* utilizes GLBT while the *Gay, Lesbian and Straight Education Network* (GLSEN) utilizes LGBT.

(RE)EVALUATING GENDER/ED REALITIES

introduction

The cases in this section show individuals who feel a need to *(re)evaluate gender/ed realities*. In these cases, the characters are stuck at a crossroads (i.e., negotiating parenting, marriage, work-life balance, etc.) and so they must evaluate and/or reevaluate what their decision means for their gender/ed reality.

 Dan's Question: Can Two Gay White Men Successfully Parent a Three-Year-Old African American Girl?, by Kathleen M. Galvin and Dennis Patrick

 Money *or* Family/Money *for* Family: Fatherhood Dilemmas for Men of Differing Socioeconomic Classes, by Suzy D'Enbeau, Patrice Buzzanell, and John Duckworth

 "You Don't Just *Not* Get Married": The Normalization of Gender Role Expectations, by Karen L. Daas

"This Just Isn't Working Out": Gender, Technology, and Work/Family, by Annis G. Golden

Undercover Moms, Family CEOs, and "Opt-Out Revolution" Moms: Work-Life Possibilities for Women, by Erika L. Kirby and M. Chad McBride

 "I Feel like I Won't be a Good Mom if I Don't at Least *Try*": The Breastfeeding Debate, by Sherianne Shuler

Dan's Question: Can Two Gay White Men Successfully Parent a Three-Year-Old African-American Girl?

Kathleen M. Galvin and Dennis Patrick

KEY TERMS

- ◆ mothering/fathering
- ◆ sexual orientation
- ◆ homophobia
- ◆ adoption
- ◆ race/ethnicity

Can two, gay, white men successfully parent a three-year-old African-American girl? That question has been bouncing around inside Dan's head for the last few days as he and his partner Tony argued the pros and cons of this possibility. He thought to himself, "Talk about making a commitment! In a few days we will make a decision that will impact our lives dramatically, no matter how the question is resolved, and in some ways I am surprised to be faced with this question in the first place. I never thought I could or would be a parent. Never. Not in a million years. In my mind, being gay and being a parent just didn't go together."

Dan remembered back to 12 years ago, when he was asked to be a guardian for his sister's kids if anything happened to her, and felt he could not agree to do it, believing it would be unfair to the kids. It hurt Dan to tell Jasmine that he could not take on that responsibility, but it seemed the right thing to do at the time. "Boy things can change," Dan thought. "Now I might be a parent myself." Feeling a need to talk these issues out with someone other than Tony, upon the recommendation of a friend, Dan was seeking the advice of a local social worker with expertise in foster care and adoption issues. He took the elevator to the fourth floor and entered Alicia Stanton's waiting room, where an administrative assistant promptly ushered him into her office.

After he had settled into the couch and they had shared some "small talk," Ms. Stanton began: "Well, Dan, let's start at the beginning. Since I know part of our conversation will lead to being a parent, I'd like to hear about your own childhood."

"Well, I was born and raised in a small town in rural Nebraska in a family of four kids. Dad ran an insurance company, and Mom worked part time at a local restaurant. Most people looked similar and everyone knew everyone else. The whole town turned out for football games and parades, and almost everyone belonged to one of the three Protestant churches in town. Throughout adolescence I realized I was different from my buddies; I had many more female friends and sometimes became uncomfortable with the guys. Dating wasn't a big thing for me but I hung out with a mixed group of friends and tried to fit in. In that place and time the only way I heard about homosexuals was when my friends used slurs, such as 'Don't be such a faggot' or 'That outfit makes you look like a dyke,' which made me really uncomfortable. There were times when I wished I could talk about my feelings with a teacher or pastor, but I never had the guts to open my mouth. To my knowledge, I grew up not knowing anyone who was gay or lesbian, or anyone even just struggling with issues of sexual orientation. It never even occurred to me that gays or lesbians lived in long-term relationships or could become parents."

"And so how did life change for you once you moved away from your hometown?"

Dan smiled. "My world became much wider when I went to college at Midwestern state university. I encountered all kinds of diversity—racial, religious, and sexual. In college, I stumbled across a GLBT[1] (gay-lesbian-bisexual-transgender) student organization during my sophomore year. During my junior year, I started to hang out with a guy from the organization and our conversations led me to fully realize and accept my sexual orientation. I eventually came out to friends during my senior year, but I did not come out to my family until a few years later. After graduation, I moved to Chicago to teach in a large suburban school district with a diverse student body and faculty. I started to attend some events in downtown Chicago for gays. I dated and had a few close relationships, but nothing really serious. Then I met my partner, Tony. We've been together 10 years now."

"Tell me about Tony." Ms. Stanton encouraged.

"I met Tony when we were both volunteers for a gay film festival in the city. Tony is from Chicago and is a physical therapist and talented jazz musician. He came out to his friends in high school and to his family in college. Most of his family was supportive and they'd included Tony's first partner in all family gatherings.

We dated for a year and then moved in together. For the first few years, I referred to Tony as my 'roommate' and, when my family members would come to Chicago, Tony was conveniently out-of-town. Eventually, I told my sister, Jasmine, and my mother. They broke the news to the other family members. A few were not shocked, but my father took it very hard. We still try to avoid talking about the subject openly.

"When we first became partners, Tony and I talked a lot about what a commitment would mean when there was no option for a ceremony or a legal process to join us. We also discussed how much we would miss being fathers, but that we would try to be good uncles to a growing set of nieces and nephews. Tony has a big local family so we interact with those kids very frequently. We're the uncles who babysit for weekends and take the kids to parades, movies, and the Lincoln Park Zoo. We attend birthday parties and First Communions because we both love kids. It was the reason I majored in elementary education. I genuinely enjoy going to work every day. A number of parents have told me I'm the best teacher their son or daughter has ever had."

Ms. Stanton interjected, "Well, that is quite the compliment, Dan!"

"It is, but I've come to realize that one of the reasons identifying as a gay man was such a struggle for me was because I thought I would never *be* a parent myself. The few gay men I knew who were parents had been married, had kids, divorced, and then came out. Over time, I made some lesbian friends who became parents through the artificial insemination of one partner, but obviously that was not a path gay men could follow. Five years ago, we contacted a surrogate parenting agency but quickly learned the fees were much more than we could afford. Eventually we resigned ourselves to the fact that we just weren't meant to be parents. We grew comfortable with that decision and our lives continued as usual, but then life changed."

"How so?" Ms. Stanton inquired.

"Three summers ago I was introduced to a new faculty member, Kathy, at the school where I teach. We quickly became good friends. Kathy and her husband are the parents of four boys they adopted through the foster-care system. Tony and I grew close to the whole family and began to watch the children one night a month so Kathy and her husband could have a night out.

One day, Kathy said, 'You're terrific with our kids. You really ought to investigate becoming foster parents. There are always more children in the system than families willing to care for them.' After that conversation, Tony and I often stayed up well into the night, talking about the possibility of foster parenting. We asked each other, 'Could we handle being separated from a child who was returned to his or her birth family? Could we really accept a dramatic change to our comfortable lifestyle? Could we parent children with special needs? Could we parent children from different racial backgrounds?' We ultimately decided it was worth a try, knowing that if it turned out to be more than we could handle we were not making any permanent commitments. We discussed our plans at length with Tony's family because they lived nearby and would be affected by our decision. They encouraged us to apply."

"So tell me about how your experiences as foster parents have been going."

"The first decision Tony and I faced was whether to disclose or hide our relationship from the foster care and adoption agency. We chose the same agency that Kathy and her husband used because they had such a positive experience working with them. This particular agency happened to be a church-based private agency. My fear was that the agency would reject our application to become foster parents if they knew we were gay. We ultimately decided not to disclose our relationship to them. So I applied for a foster-care license as a single man and listed Tony as a roommate sharing my house. We're still not sure that was the right decision to make. We think Ramona, our case manager who did the home study, suspected we were more than just roommates, but she seemed to be operating under a 'don't ask, don't tell' policy. It was hard for me to pretend that Tony and I were simply friends because we are out in every other aspect of our lives. I'm not necessarily proud of what we did, but Tony reassured me that, with so many children in care waiting for families, the end justified the means.

"Once we—I mean, once I—got my foster care license, Ramona promised that it would not be long before I got my first placement. She was right. The phone call came less than two weeks later. The agency was looking for a placement for two Latino brothers, ages six and eight, whose mother was in a residential drug rehabilitation program. Mario and Raul joined us for nine months until their mother was able to reclaim them. Although the boys were very shy and uncomfortable at first, we soon learned that Mario had a wonderful sense of humor and Raul loved to sing and perform. We had to talk with teachers, meet other parents from the school, and change our grocery list! Our families were supportive and the boys got along well with Tony's nephews. It turned out to be a wonderful and stressful experience, so when the time came for them to rejoin their mother, it was very difficult to let them go. Tony and I talked about it and decided to continue as foster parents."

"That must have been a hard decision; how many children have you had in your care since then?"

"Soon after the boys left, the agency sent us a number of children for short-term placements. We had a 10-year-old boy, 12-year-old female twins, a four-year-old boy who was battling leukemia, and a number of other weekend or month-long placements. The agency staff called us often because the children seemed to be comfortable in our home; we were flexible about placements and we did not need excessive agency support.

"Over time, we revealed we were a same-sex couple to Ramona. She laughed and said, 'Don't worry, I already know and have absolutely no problem with it.' She added, 'It might cause some problems with the agency though so maybe it's best to continue to refer to Tony as a roommate in my files and reports as you build your credibility as a foster father.' That was 18 months ago. For the last six months, we have been fostering a three-year-old African-American girl named Keisha. She calls me 'Daddy' and Tony 'Papa.' She loves to sing, dance, and tell stories. Her laughter is contagious and her smile lights up the room. Last week she said, 'I love you, Daddy' for the very first time and my heart melted."

"How sweet," said Ms. Stanton, "there is nothing like a child's expression of love."

"True . . . but I wasn't quite ready to feel so attached, and then three days ago Ramona called and said, 'Keisha's birth mother has made the decision to voluntarily terminate her parental rights. Since there are no biological relatives who are able or willing to care for her, the agency is seeking an adoptive family.' She wanted to know if we were interested in adopting Keisha. I was incredibly excited as well as incredibly anxious. This decision would be a major commitment, one that would change our lives in many ways. Once again, Tony and I were up late into the night, debating the question constantly occupying my thoughts: 'Can two gay white men successfully parent an African-American girl?'"

Ms. Stanton asked quietly, "And how are you answering that question, Dan?"

"Well, Tony and I had done a lot of research on gay parenting before making the decision to get our foster-care license. During that process we were exposed to the views of individuals who are opposed to same sex couples raising kids, no matter how the kids came into their lives. These feelings seem to be far stronger for gay male parents than for lesbian parents, and we've heard similar objections from some of my siblings. One of the toughest issues we've encountered involves the common belief that every child, but especially a girl child, *must* have a mother. We struggle with this also.

"Our friends, Eric and Jack, used a surrogate and now have two school-aged girls. When their family went places together while the girls were little, strangers assumed one parent was the Dad and the other was an uncle or friend. They encountered strangers' friendly comments about, 'Mom's night out' or 'Mom's time off' from people in restaurants or in parks. As the girls grew older and could understand the conversations, Eric and Jack began to respond that they were the parents. Some strangers looked horrified and walked away without a word. A number blurted out things like, 'Every child needs a mother.' They've consciously enlisted Eric's mother and sister and Jack's best friend, Sarah, to be extensively involved with the girls to help ease the concerns about not having a mother. But Jack's sister *still* scolds them that 'growing up with two fathers will cause the girls to be confused about their own identities and/or sexual orientation.'"

"So are you implying that this would be easier to figure out if Keisha was a little boy?"

"In some ways I do think it would be easier, although that would have its own issues because some people believe gay men are more likely to be child molesters—a horrendous stereotype. Although there is no research or evidence to support that belief, it's troubling that some people would think that of us. What is particularly hard is that some close friends and relatives—including my sister, Jasmine, and some members of Tony's family—honestly believe it would be unfair to Keisha. They argue that same-sex parents will cause a child to be teased or ostracized by peers or neighbors, putting her on the defensive in multiple situations. They also wonder if Keisha would regret being in such a household after she is grown.

"Another issue of concern involves interracial adoption. We would be a family formed through 'visible' adoption, meaning that it would always be clear that we have no biological ties to our daughter, as is the case when Caucasians adopt children from China or Vietnam. But it's more complicated when Caucasian parents adopt African-American children in the United States. We've read about it being a controversial issue since 1972 when the National Association of Black Social Workers formally declared its opposition to the placement of African-American children with white parents. Although such placements do occur, they are less frequent and somewhat controversial. The issue mainly relates to the ability of Caucasians to socialize African-American children into their ethnic culture and to prepare them for difficulties they might encounter in U.S. society."

"How are you feeling about your ability to deal with those difficulties? I think if anyone would be prepared to take on that challenge, a teacher from a diverse Chicago school would."

"I don't see this as an insurmountable issue, but Tony seems to think it is quite significant. He's worrying about whether we can prepare Keisha for all she will face as a young African-American woman in our society. He's worried about how other kids will relate to her. Although some of our friends are not direct about it, they appear to disapprove of the idea, saying 'Kids need parents who look like them.' Clearly, in this case, Keisha might not 'look' like many of her family or friends—given two white dads!

"But what's most frustrating is our inability to really know the answer to 'What if . . .' We have no way to know, and have no say in, where Keisha might be placed if we refuse the offer to adopt. We have grown to love her and care deeply about her. And she is very attached to us, and we know we would provide a good, secure home. Ramona has given us a week to come to a decision. After we put Keisha to bed tonight, Tony and I will be up talking and trying to answer the question we can't get out of our heads, and the question that led me to you, Ms. Stanton: 'Can two, gay, white men successfully parent an African-American girl?'"

endnote

1. GLBT (also LGBT): either of these expressions are acronyms for individuals who are gay, lesbian, bisexual, or transgender/transsexual. The acronym differs across organizations; for example, the Human Rights Campaign (HRC) utilizes GLBT while the Gay, Lesbian and Straight Education Network (GLSEN) utilizes LGBT.

19

Money *or* Family/Money *for* Family

Fatherhood Dilemmas for Men of Differing Socioeconomic Classes

Suzy D'Enbeau, Patrice Buzzanell,
and John Duckworth

KEY TERMS

- ♦ (good) fathering
- ♦ work-life balance
- ♦ masculinity
- ♦ socioeconomic class
- ♦ caregiving

It was "Dads and Donuts Day" for a new school year at Parkview Elementary School, and Kenny Johnson raced down the street in a rush to get to the school on time. This annual meeting provided a space for fathers of elementary school students to connect with the school, with each other, and with their children through a variety of learning activities. The kids waited patiently with their teachers and then would excitedly meet their dads in the gym after school. In addition to the interactive games the fathers and children played, fathers could also sign up to help with afterschool activities throughout the year. The agenda for this meeting also covered the additional expenses of afterschool activities such as soccer practice, music lessons, and dance team. Kenny's three daughters really wanted to be involved in these activities.

Kenny always enjoyed this event but lately he had a lot on his mind. As he pulled up at the school, he thought of a cell phone conversation with his wife that he had on the drive from work to the school. He remembered why he had called Alice in the first place: "Remind me when I get home tonight we need to have sort of a serious talk. Remember that Sheila asked me whether or not I want to add more overtime hours, and I said I would get back to her. Well, I need an answer by Friday. In some ways, it seems like a no-brainer . . . we could use the money for all the kids' activities—those costs add up fast."

"It sounds like you are leaning toward taking it, but don't forget that spending time with the kids is also important, and if you take those hours you will see the kids less," Alice replied.

Kenny rushed into the gym and scanned the room for his girls. They ran up to him and the four grabbed seats in the back just as the events were beginning. He took a nametag from the back table, quickly scribbled his name with a black marker, and stuck the tag to his Carhart shirt. He wiped the sweat from his brow. He caught their glances and smiled at his daughters. Then he reviewed his dilemma one more time, weighing pros and cons yet still not coming up with a satisfactory answer: "We could really use the money so the kids can be involved in after school activities this year. But if I work more, I will see my family even less. Should I add more hours so we have more money? Or is it more important that I spend time with my family? Which is a better measure of a good father?"[1]

Until recently, Kenny had not given much thought to working less and being home more with his family. As a forklift operator at Paper, Inc., Kenny worked 40 hours per week. The laboring was hard on his body, and combined with the travel time to and from work, he was gone about 10 hours a day. This schedule had never been a problem. Alice worked part time so she was able to be home when their three children got home from school. Kenny had never seen a problem with Alice providing more daily care for their kids; after all, his mom stayed home and took care of Kenny and his siblings while his dad was responsible for supporting the family financially. And he attended "Dads and Donuts Day" every year.

But today's morning newspaper had highlighted Alice's sentiment about fatherhood being more than financial support. The headline declared, "What it means to be a good father." According to the article, "to meet the growing demands of today's families, fathers must add caregiving responsibilities to their already present role of breadwinner." In other words, good fathers are able to balance their financial and caregiving responsibilities. They not only work but also are willing and able to spend time at home with their families on a regular basis. Kenny had to admit this was something he and Alice had been talking about a lot lately. When she took a new job as a nurse's aid for a senior center, the couple had discussed Kenny cutting back his work hours and taking more responsibility with their three school-aged kids. And he was looking forward to that—he wanted to be there to help his kids with homework, attend school events, and have meals together. Just last night at dinner, his oldest daughter said to him, "Daddy, will you sign up to be a coach for my soccer team this year? I really, really want you to be there to help me play." Kenny wanted to help coach the team but he did not see how they could afford the additional expenses of his daughters' activities if he did not add overtime.

As a teacher stepped forward to the podium, a glaring siren pierced the gym. Someone shouted, "It's a tornado drill!" With that, the teachers who helped coordinate the day gathered the children while the parents in the gym began to make their way through the doors, into the hallway, and down the stairs to the basement. Kenny silently followed along. As he situated himself in the basement, he took a seat on the floor near a group of other fathers.

"I wonder if this is a drill or if there's really a tornado? I can't afford for this to be just a drill. I had to rearrange my whole work schedule to make this meeting today," Dale explained.

"I know what you mean," Kenny sighed. "I was rushing to make it here on time." As the kids were kept preoccupied with some teacher-initiated activities, six men had haphazardly formed a circle on the hallway floor—some leaning against the wall, others squatting, and still others folded up with their arms wrapped around their legs, seemingly afraid to rub up too close to the grime of the basement or to brush up against the other men. Kenny recognized their faces and names, and knew these fathers' kids were friends with his kids. If he coached the soccer team, he may even get to work with their daughters. He looked down at the floor while an awkward silence permeated the air. Then George sparked a conversation.

"Hey, did you all see the headline in today's Lifestyle section of the paper? Something about what it means to be a good father?" asked George. The group mumbled in disgruntled agreement. "You know, I just feel like I can't win at being a father. Don't get me wrong—I love to be with my kid. But sometimes I can't find the time with my work schedule as a janitor."

"You know," Ryan interjected, "I read that article and thought to myself that I also really wish we could spend more time together as a family. My wife and I both work quite a bit. She's a surgeon and with my law practice, we struggle to spend time with our twins. We manage to get in quality time on the weekends. And thank goodness for our nanny. She has really helped us out. My wife's friends said, 'Don't let her get away,' when we had the opportunity to hire her. She's the only one we interviewed, and we hired her then right away. She's been so good about staying late when we need her to. My wife works late, and I'm the president of a local community group. We feel it's important for our kids to see how involved we are with work and community organizations to set a good example for them, to let them know that they can be leaders, too. Getting involved in extracurricular school activities is one way for them to begin their involvement with outside organizations."

Ryan made a good point, Kenny thought to himself. He wanted his kids to see that he could be a good leader for activities and events that were about them—like coaching the soccer team. But Ryan's situation was different. Kenny certainly did not have the income of a lawyer; he and Alice could not afford to hire a nanny. Besides, Kenny thought that hiring a nanny did not necessarily make a person a good father. Someone else would still be providing the care. Kenny wondered how he could help Alice more with the kids, add more leadership responsibilities, and increase his hours at work.

Alice had questioned Kenny about whether adding overtime would really benefit the family. She was always good at playing the devil's advocate, and so Kenny had talked to his coworker, Lisa, about his dilemma. Lisa had recently added overtime hours to pay for bills and to help put her kids through college. Lisa explained, "You know, if I didn't work overtime here, I would probably have to get a second job. The money's great but absence does make the heart grow fonder. I miss spending time with my family. But when I do get to see them, I'm so tired that all I want to do is sleep." Later Lisa explained, "I pump myself up to get through it. If I get discouraged or the time seems to be dragging by, I remind myself how much we need the money. I think about the bills coming in. I think of my kids going to college."

Kenny had heard stories like Lisa's and others about dealing with the demands of overtime. He recalled long-circulating rumors at Paper, Inc. about how many workers had simply become exhausted by the demanding physical energy required of them. He had heard stories of workers who resorted to using drugs to help them stay awake on the job so they would not fall asleep using the machines. They would use drugs to stay awake, but then they eventually became addicted so that they could not work without using the drugs. Other workers bargained with themselves. They said things like, "If I just keep putting in these extra hours and working 6–7 days a week, my kids will be able to go to college and get jobs that won't require them to work overtime. They'll have salaries and be able to balance their work with their family."

They talked about other issues as well. Some workers' situations were complicated by divorce. Kenny remembered what his coworker Tomas had said the other day at lunch. Tomas had cut his overtime hours from 110 to 50 hours a month because of his divorce. He explained, "The whole reason I ended up divorced in the first place was because of working all the time. And now that we're divorced, I need more overtime to make child support payments since those payments are calculated based on my base pay and overtime. It's a vicious cycle that I can't seem to get out of!" Although Kenny did not expect that he and Alice would divorce, he was concerned that working more would cause them to grow apart. If he added more hours at work, he hoped that his marriage would not suffer like Tomas'.

Kenny's thoughts returned to his situation in the basement of the school. He shifted his weight because his right leg was getting cramped. As he was doing so, he listened as Dale explained his situation, "My wife and I recently divorced, and I have to admit, the past year has been really difficult. My ex has made visitation a real issue—she tells me when I have to pick the kids up and when I have to drop them off. She really demands a lot of flexibility from my schedule that I don't always have. As a case manager at the local shelter, I don't work a typical 9 to 5 job. I'm on call during the evenings and weekends, and she makes it challenging for me to have the kids. But if I don't keep this job, I won't have enough money for child support, bills, and being able to take the kids out for pizza when they visit." Kenny and Alice also still liked to be able to take the kids out for dinner every once and awhile. But lately, they did not seem to have enough money for activities like that.

Carl had yet to share his story. The other five fathers turned to face him. "My wife works full time, and I stay home with our kids. When we first married, we both had full-time jobs. But as a college professor, she was making more money than my job as an event planner for a local nonprofit. When we decided to start our family, we knew that we didn't want to pay for childcare. We felt it was important to have one parent home with the kids. And her job has really taken off. I love being home with the kids so I was happy to do it, but when I see some of the other moms at the park or at the bus stop, they act a little funny around me. I've heard them make comments about my wife being too career driven. But we're happy with our decision. And I always love meeting other dads at 'Dads and Donuts Day.'" The other men just nodded while looking away. Most of them had not met a man who enjoyed staying home full time with the kids. Kenny could not imagine staying home with the kids even if they could afford it. It had never occurred to him to reverse the traditional roles of men and women. It seemed unnatural.

George sat up. "You know, personally, I think it's great that you get to spend so much time with your kids, Carl. I'm a single dad so I get to see my son quite a bit, but for me, it's not just about being able to see my son. On my off days, I have to also take care of my father." George continued, "I'm a janitor Monday, Tuesday, Thursday, and Saturday. I have my son on Wednesdays and Fridays, but my father was just diagnosed with cancer so I have to take care of him as well. I try to relax on my off days but it just doesn't seem possible. At the same time, I try to get in overtime when possible to help out my dad. Sometimes I resent that working overtime means I have less time with my dad but I need the money to help him." Kenny thought about George's situation. Not only did he have to provide financial and caregiving support for his son, but to be a good father, he also had to care for his own father.

"It's funny hearing the way you all talk about today's newspaper article," Bryce sheepishly said. "I read that article, too, and thought 'finally, an article that calls on men to take more responsibility for their children.' I mean, I work full time as a graphic designer. I'm lucky that I can set my own schedule and can often work from home. For our first child, my wife worked and we had a nanny. But with our second child, we decided as a family that it would be most beneficial to us that one of us stay home. We thought that usually it's the mom who stays home but we also looked at both of our careers and felt it would probably be better if I continued to work and she stayed at home with the kids as their primary caregiver. Our situation has really worked out well. My wife is able to be involved with lots of the kids' activities. And I help out when I can." Kenny wondered what that would be like. He and Alice had never given much thought to one of them staying home full time. It just never seemed like a feasible option. It always seemed like they needed more money—money for school, money to go out to dinner, money to go the movies, money for new toys. The idea of having *enough* money was always in the distance.

Kenny recalled his sister's reaction when they talked on his way into work that morning, and he told her about the news article about being a good father. Colleen was dismayed, "You know it seems like families with lower incomes are less likely to have fathers who are successful caregivers *and* primary financial breadwinners. For parents like Howard and me, the choice is not money *or* family but money *for* family." Kenny could understand her viewpoint. Her husband Howard worked long hours at the local car factory while she worked nights at a detox center. Between their two jobs, they could barely make ends meet but at least she was able to be home with the kids during the day. It always made Colleen angry to hear stories about women who choose to stay home with the kids. She would exclaim, "Most families don't have the choice!"

Kenny's thoughts drifted back to the basement of Parkview Elementary School. Fathers were starting to get up and move around. The tornado drill was over, and people were filing up the stairs and back into the gym. As Kenny followed the crowd, he continued to debate his dilemma in his head. "Should I ask for more overtime? If I ask for the hours, work will keep me away from my family even more. But if I don't add the overtime, I don't see how Alice and I can provide for our family. What does it mean to be a good father? And how can I become a good father? Should I coach my daughter's soccer team or work more to make sure that all of the girls can participate in afterschool activities? To be a 'good father,' is it better to provide money for kids' activities or to be able to go to those activities?"

endnote

1. This case context is fictional but the fathers' life circumstances and quotes are derived from actual interviews conducted for John Duckworth's unpublished M.A. thesis, *The discourse and practice of fatherhood: Identity negotiations of masculinities, caregiving, and work-family issues,* completed at Purdue University in West Lafayette, Indiana in 2006, and winner of the 2007 Outstanding Thesis Award from the Organization for the Study of Communication, Language and Gender. Other quotes and circumstances are derived from academic journal and research articles on work, parenting, and class.

"You Don't Just *Not* Get Married"

The Normalization of Gender Role Expectations

Karen L. Daas

Kelly stepped out of her car with hesitation. Her friends would want to know what had happened on her date with Mitch last night, and she was not sure she wanted to share the details. She knew this was supposed to be the happiest moment in her life, but it did not quite feel that way. She had certainly been surprised when Mitch proposed over their dessert, but she had been even more surprised when she realized that she was not sure she wanted to accept the proposal. They had been dating for three years and marriage seemed like the next logical step. Still, she wondered why she did not feel like it was a step she was excited to take. She took a deep breath and headed into the coffee shop.

As soon as she reached the table, Maria asked, "So, what happened last night? I tried to call you after class, but you didn't answer. Don't tell me he broke up with you."

"No, he didn't break up with me," Kelly responded. "He asked me to marry him."

"Wow!" Maria squealed. "Congratulations! Did you talk about a date? You should have it at the country club next fall. I had my wedding there. My pictures were so beautiful, with the mountains in the background and the lake. They have that lovely fountain and . . ."

". . . Maria, we know . . . we were there. We'll get to that in a minute," interrupted Jessica. "Kelly, let me see the ring."

"I don't have it," Kelly said.

"Why not? What kind of guy asks you to marry him and doesn't give you a ring?" inquired Jessica. "Jay showed me the ring before he even asked me. Otherwise, there is no way I would have said yes. Come to think of it, I don't remember what he said since I was so busy staring at my ring." Jessica paused for a moment to study her ring and show it once again to the others at the table, even though they had all seen it numerous times in the three weeks since Jessica had become engaged. "I knew as soon as he showed me this ring that he loves me. I can't even imagine how much he spent. I know they're supposed to spend the equivalent of their salary for two months, but I know he spent much more than that. If that doesn't say love, I don't know what does. Sorry, I'm getting off track. Let's get back to you. Where is your ring?"

Kelly hesitated as she planned her response. "Well," she finally offered, "Mitch has it for now."

Jessica looked confused. "Why did he show it to you if he wasn't going to give it to you? That's just mean of him to tease you with it. Or is it really ugly or something and he has to return it?"

"No, it's not ugly," Kelly replied. "But I'm just not sure I want it right now."

"What is wrong with it? Does he need to have it sized or something? What other reason could there be? I'm so confused," Jessica offered as she tried to make sense of the situation.

"Whatever the ring looks like, it's okay," Maria tried to soothe Kelly. "The important thing is that you love him and he loves you. If the ring is small or not what you wanted, you can always upgrade later. When Matt and I got engaged, he only paid about $500 for my ring. It was all he could afford and fine for the time, but then, for our first anniversary, he bought me a really beautiful ring. He had started working at the law firm by then. I still have the original in my jewelry box because it has sentimental value for me, but I *love* this ring."

"It's not about the ring," Kelly finally confessed. "The ring is beautiful and I don't care how much it costs."

"Does it look like the one you have in your book?" Ashley interrupted.

"What book are you talking about?" Maria questioned. "Have I seen the book? Should I know what you're talking about?"

Kelly was quiet for a moment, thinking about Ashley's question. She knew exactly the book Ashley was talking about.

Ashley and Kelly had grown up together. They had been neighbors, classmates, and best friends for as long as she could remember. They used to play wedding with their dolls and sometimes even played dress-up, using curtains for veils as they pretended to walk down the aisle with twin brothers. At that age, Ashley and Kelly planned on marrying twins so that they could become sisters-in-law and guarantee that they really would be friends forever.

When they were in junior high and feeling too old to play with dolls, they each started a bridal book. They would cut pictures out of magazines or write down ideas of what they wanted for their perfect wedding based on what they had seen in movies and on television. They had even taken pictures at Ashley's older sister's wedding and cut out the parts they wanted for their own. They had given up the idea of marrying twins since they did not know any, but Ashley had taken to cutting out pictures of men she thought she could marry and creating entire stories in which she gave the men personalities and planned her life. First there was the big wedding, then the children, and finally, happily ever after.

When Ashley began obsessing about the image of the perfect man, Kelly began to shy away from working on her bridal book. She feared that Ashley had set up unrealistic expectations, and she did not want to find herself in a similar situation. At one time, Ashley had even confided in Kelly that she had the perfect wedding planned and would begin to make formal arrangements once she found a guy to fit into her vision. When Kelly asked how Ashley would know the guy, Ashley responded that it did not really matter who the guy was as long as he went along with Ashley's plans. This confession had caused fear in Kelly as she began to think that Ashley might be alone forever, and she tried to introduce new activities that would keep Ashley's mind off of the bridal book. Kelly's reluctance to fantasize about their weddings had put a strain on her friendship with Ashley, which began to deteriorate more when Kelly started dating and Ashley started spending too much time alone. They had remained friends throughout high school and now college, but Ashley seemed to resent Kelly, especially once she had started dating Mitch seriously.

Despite the fact that Kelly had not pulled out her bridal book in almost five years, she knew exactly where she had stored it and, more importantly, the ring to which Ashley was referring. It had been in an advertisement for a three-stone ring with channel set diamonds. The woman in the picture looked so happy, as if she could never love anyone more and she knew that she would be happy for the rest of her life. Kelly knew a ring could not promise happiness—it certainly had not for her parents, who had divorced when she was eight—but something about the woman's eyes as she stared at that ring and rested on her fiancé's shoulder made Kelly think that an engagement ring was definitely a step in the right direction.

Coming back to the present, Kelly answered Ashley. "No, it doesn't look like that ring . . . it's a bit simpler . . . but that's not why I don't have it." She could not help but wonder if the understated ring had contributed to her decision at some level. She did love Mitch and did not think the ring mattered, but she was a little disappointed with the style he had chosen.

Beyond the ring, though, Kelly was a little disappointed with the proposal as a whole. Not only was she not expecting Mitch to propose, but she was also not anticipating that he would do so in such a cliché manner. Had he never watched any of the proposal reality shows on television? Did he really think there was no better option than during dessert at a fancy restaurant? And why would he propose now, when they were months away from graduation and neither of them could barely afford their own apartments let alone a nice wedding or a house? She had really expected more from him.

"Hello? Kelly," Jessica pulled her out of her thoughts. "I'd still like to know why you're not wearing your ring."

"Because I haven't decided if I'm going to marry him," Kelly stated.

"Why wouldn't you marry him?" Maria asked. "You two have been together almost three years."

"I know. We have been together a long time," Kelly replied. "But I still do not feel like I am ready to marry him. I have been enjoying the relationship that we have. I am not sure I am ready for it to change. What if it is a mistake to marry him now?"

"Do you think there's someone better out there?" Ashley probed.

"It is not that," Kelly responded. "I have not even thought about whether there might be someone else for me. Actually, when I think about the future, I can see Mitch and me together. The thing is that I am just not sure that I want to get married."

"I don't understand you at all," Ashley interjected. "You are so lucky to have someone who wants to marry you. Why would you say no? I don't even have a boyfriend. I would *kill* to be in your shoes."

"I wish you were in my shoes," Kelly said. "It's not that I don't love Mitch or that I think there's someone better out there. I'm just not sure marriage is for me and I'm almost certain that it's definitely not right for me at this time in my life. I want to go to graduate school and maybe join the Peace Corps. I'm not sure I could do all of that if I were married."

"But just think how wonderful it would be if we could plan our weddings together," coaxed Jessica. "You could help me plan mine and once mine is over, we'll start planning yours. I'll be able to give you all sorts of tips. Maybe we could even shop together and get some deals if we both agree to use the same photographer or caterer or . . ."

"Jess, can we talk about whether she is going to get married before we start trying to plan a double wedding," Ashley interrupted.

"For your information, I am not talking about a double wedding," Jessica responded harshly. "As much as I love you, Kelly, I am not sharing my day."

"You need to think about someone other than yourself for a minute," Ashley sighed with frustration. "Kelly, have you thought about what might happen if you say no? Mitch might be really upset or, worse yet, he might break up with you. What if he breaks up with you? You never know if you're going to meet someone new. You could be alone the rest of your life. Doesn't that scare you?"

"Yes. No. I don't know." Kelly began to scan the faces of her friends. She wanted their advice, but she needed to make sure that what she decided was based on *her* needs rather than her friends' opinions. "I appreciate all of your advice, but I need to think about this. And I need to think about what to tell Mitch. I don't want to break up with him, but I'm only 22 and I don't want to get married right now. I still have so much to do with my life."

"Well, you could always have a long engagement," Ashley offered.

"Oh, good idea," Maria said. "Matt and I were engaged for a year before we were married. That gave me plenty of time to plan my wedding and start working on how we would combine our furniture. He had a hideous coffee table."

"You'll have to tell me how you managed to get rid of that," Jessica said. "Jay has this ugly chair that does not match any of my furniture. I do not want him moving that thing into our new apartment."

Kelly, becoming truly frustrated, lashed out, "I don't think you are listening to me. I am not concerned about a long engagement or furniture. I just don't feel like I want to get married . . . definitely not now and maybe not ever."

Ashley gasped. The friends sat silently at the table for a moment before Jessica spoke. "I understand your fears. They are only natural. I was scared to death when Jay showed me the box, but as I thought about how much I love him, I knew that marrying him was the right thing to do. I could not imagine my life without him, so why would I give him the chance to get away?"

"I felt the same way when Matt proposed to me," Maria confirmed. "It is a big change to get married, but it is such an achievement to be able to spend the rest of your life with someone. To hear you say that you do not feel like you want to get married, that is your fear talking, not your heart."

"I appreciate that both of you are happy being married or almost married," Kelly said, "but why are you trying to push me into this? Do you understand that I want something different for myself? I thought you were my friends."

"We are your friends," Maria stated with a touch of hurt in her voice. "We're just trying to keep you from doing something that you might regret. Have you really thought about what it means to turn down a proposal? That could be really bad for your relationship."

"I suppose it could," Kelly conceded, "although I would like to think that Mitch knows me well enough to understand. I don't understand why it is so important to get married. Does it mean that I'm not committed if I'm not married?"

"It's that you don't just *not* get married," Ashley concluded. "You're a woman and that's what you are supposed to do. If you don't want to get married, then what is the point of dating in the first place? It doesn't make sense to run the race if you don't want to win it."

"I agree," Maria said. "So what are you going to tell Mitch?"

Kelly closed her eyes and began to think about all of the things she had been told since she was a young girl. She always thought she would get married and have children someday, but now that the question had been asked, she had no idea how to answer it. She knew she would be running into Mitch later that afternoon . . .

"This Just Isn't Working Out"
Gender, Technology, and Work/Family

Annis G. Golden

KEY TERMS

- work and family/gendered division of domestic labor
- gendered impacts of information and communication technologies
- intersectionality of gender and ethnicity

Riya put her 10 month-old son, Atul, in the playpen next to her computer in the living room. At 6:30 in the evening, she had fed Atul and herself, and she was ready to pick up where she had left off when she checked out of the Engineering Department at InfoTech for the day at 3:00 P.M. Sitting down at the computer, she felt stressed: "The deadline for the new product release is looming, and the coding isn't going as smoothly as I'd hoped." Dinner was in the oven for her husband, Deepak, keeping warm until he arrived home at 8:00 P.M. Riya logged on to the InfoTech intranet and returned to the project.[1]

It was not easy to concentrate on the coding with Atul bouncing in his playpen right next to her, but she managed. If she put him in the next room, he would howl for her attention, and then she could not get anything done. "Deepak will take over when he gets home," she thought, but that was rarely before 8:00 P.M. He had tried coming home earlier and doing some of his work at home through his company's network, but he said he got so little done that it was much more efficient to stay there later and then focus completely on Atul when he got home.

When she was pregnant with Atul, Riya and Deepak had talked at length about how they would manage once the baby was born. Riya's mother would be coming over from India to help for the first few months, but after that, they would be on their own. Riya loved her work as a software engineer at InfoTech, and over the four years she had worked there, Jim, the director of her department, had clearly communicated to her that she was a valued contributor. Deepak supported her desire to keep working after the baby arrived, but they both agreed they did not want to have the baby in daycare 10 hours a day. So Riya asked Jim if she could use InfoTech's reduced work week program and go to 80 percent time after she returned from maternity leave. Jim readily agreed, and for the past seven months, Riya had been coming in at 9:00 A.M. and leaving at 3:00 P.M.

Last week, when Riya ran into her neighbor, Sharon, she'd asked how the new setup was going. Riya said, "Well, I'm pleased with how we have things arranged for Atul—I'm so glad he doesn't have to spend 10 hours every day in daycare—but work is another story. I'm at the office 20 percent less and getting paid 20 percent less, but I'm not actually working 20 percent less and my project deadlines haven't been extended by 20 percent. They still have to be completed on the same schedules, and none of my work has been reassigned. But, you know since the layoffs two years ago, everybody in the department is busier than ever."

"And I'm sure it's hard to not get to spend all of your time with Atul," suggested Sharon.

"No, actually I'm still really passionate about my work—it's not so much that I mind doing the work . . . you know how it goes. I can log in to the intranet from home, and my computer is set up right in the living room so it's actually manageable to combine tasks like testing code with taking care of Atul. What I do mind is getting paid 80 percent for a 100 percent effort—especially when 20 percent of that effort is invisible to others in the department." Riya also worried about not participating in any of the after-work get-togethers the department organized. She did not drink, and while she did not experience any tensions working within an almost all male department, she was not entirely comfortable with the idea of going to a bar with them . . . and of course now, with the baby, it was completely out of the question. But what really bothered her most now was the idea that the other engineers might be thinking she was waltzing out of the office at 3:00 P.M. and then just relaxing the rest of the day.

"This just is not working out," Riya thought. She tried to think of what the alternatives might be. She could certainly go back to the office 100 percent time, but then Atul would be in daycare for at least two more hours a day. She could ask Jim if she could telework officially for 20 percent of her time, though she knew that there was no official organizational policy that permitted that. Besides, unofficially she had heard that it was actually frowned upon since there had been abuses of those arrangements in the past. She could ask Deepak if he could go in later or get home earlier, and do some of his work at home so that they could divide up the childcare and other household responsibilities more evenly. But while Deepak supported her work, and he had the same kind of remote access to his company's intranet as she did, he said he just could not do what she seemed to be able to do—combine work and watching Atul. "Still, this is Deepak's issue too," she told herself. "It should not be only my problem to solve. I'll talk to him tonight, and depending on what we come up with, discuss the situation with Jim."

endnote

1. This case is based on real employee and family experiences. Names, facts, and situations have been changed to protect the privacy of the individuals involved and the employing organization.

22 Undercover Moms, Family CEOs, and "Opt-Out Revolution" Moms

Work-Life Possibilities for Women

Erika L. Kirby and M. Chad McBride

KEY TERMS

- work-life balance/policy
- "doing" gender
- mothering
- (educational, white, and socioeconomic) privilege

"Boy, I love Saturdays," Andrea smiled to herself as she came down the stairs of the fitness center and guzzled the rest of her water. She had just spent two glorious hours on herself, sweating through a Butts-N-Guts class and then taking an hour of yoga. "No work, no commute, and a nice balance of time for me and time with the family . . . what a disruption to my usual routine. Saturdays make me wonder why I am still working . . ." she thought as she hit the shower and then went to grab her two-year-old twin boys, Carter and Colton, from the center's daycare. After loading them into their carseats in her trusty minivan, she headed to KidPlace. She had scheduled a playdate with her best friends from college, Brooke, and her daughter Carly, and Annabeth, and her kids Jonathan, Jacob, and Joslyn. They turned the kids loose in the ball pits and padded play structure and took a few minutes to chat.

"How was your week, Brooke?" Andrea started their familiar catch-up session.

"Same as usual. Once I'm at work, things are fine. In fact, it was a really productive week and my sales were up by 50 percent, but the stress of getting ready to take the kids to school in 'mom' clothes, then changing again before work to clothes appropriate for a pharmaceutical rep, then changing again before picking up the kids is starting to make me crazy," Brooke confessed.

"I still don't understand why you do it in the first place," Annabeth chided. "To the outside observer, it's pretty crazy."

"Well, since you stay at home with the kids, you take them to school in cute little sweat outfits and jeans. People then assume you stay at home, and they treat you a certain way . . . like you're doing 'the right thing' by spending more time with your kids. Even though I have flexible hours and am there to drop Carly off and pick her up, the few times I have worn my designer suits to school, I got all these weird looks, like the other moms were thinking, 'you think you're better than me because you work?' Of course I don't, and so being an 'undercover' working mom[1] helps me relate better to the other parents and to Carly's teachers . . . but it takes a lot of planning and changes of clothes!"

"I've heard more desperate stories . . . my cousin actually changed her hours to work at night so that she could appear to be a stay-at-home mother and yet still work," Andrea followed. But then she could just not resist teasing, "So what *did* you wear yesterday, Brooke?"

"You really get a kick out of this, huh? For your information, I wore the shell of my pink cashmere twin set under a sweatshirt to make it look like a t-shirt, and to make it easier to change in the car because I don't have to actually take my shirt off and risk flashing anyone. Then I wore jeans on the bottom with slip-on tennies that I changed out for gray wide-leg trousers and boots in the back of the minivan before I went into work . . . and I wear boy-leg panties to eliminate the potential for showing too much down low when I'm changing pants. And I added more jewelry once I left the school . . . but enough about my work hang-ups." Brooke turned to Annabeth. "How did life as a stay-at-home mom treat you this week?"

"You know I prefer the title Family CEO[2] to stay-at-home mom . . . it sounds more official and shows that I work too," Annabeth huffed, only half in jest. "Well, this week both Jake and Jos had quick spells of stomach flu, which is always a treat . . . and it seemed like all they did was bicker. Thank goodness for our pool membership so I can get them out of the house!"

"Oh come on, Annabeth. Do you really need to use that CEO title?" asked Andrea. "That seems a little over the top."

"Maybe . . . but I'm tired of not being taken seriously because I stay home with my kids instead of having a 'real job.' My brain didn't leave my body when I quit my job, you know? And it certainly *is* work to be a mom 24/7. You both have heard me fume about how I get sick of people saying what a great choice I've made . . . telling me 'A mother's care can never be replaced' or 'Staying home is the most important job in the world' but *not* really believing it. . . ." Annabeth began. "Well, just last night, I had another upsetting interaction. Shawn and I were at a party for his work and I was in a great conversation with a woman who just joined the firm about the election and the economy. We were discussing how Alaska Governor Sarah Palin was such a surprise addition to the Republican ticket for vice president and debating whether she would be taken seriously as a former PTA mom and 'hockey mom.'

"Sometimes I feel like my Master's degree doesn't get much of a workout, so it was really nice. At one point, she asked, 'Oh, I almost forgot to ask, what do you do?' and when I told her 'I stay at home with my kids,' she said, 'Oh' in a condescending tone. She then hurriedly followed with, 'I mean . . . what's someone like you doing at home?' as if that was any better. She apologized, but I'm still stinging. I work hard to raise my kids and provide a loving, comfortable home—just not for pay. I just hate when I feel like I need to justify my choice *not* to work outside the home, so half seriously and half in jest I've been trying out the Family CEO title."

Andrea mused, "How ironic . . . Brooke's changing her clothes so that people *think* she is a stay at home mother and then Annabeth gets attitude for *actually* being one. Remember that Enjoli commercial from the 1970s when we were kids? It shows a woman in three personas—suit-clad with a briefcase, robe-clad with a frying pan, and then in an evening gown singing 'I can bring home the bacon, fry it up in a pan, and never let you forget you're a man.' That and other images just set us up for failure. We aspire to be superwomen, and then feel like failures when it doesn't work out. So we take a seat on the mommy track . . . or we stay at home."

Brooke tried to add some levity to their time together. "You know, I could get this drama staying at home and watching a movie on Lifetime, you two," she joked.

Andrea and Annabeth could not help but chuckle. Then Andrea got serious. "I suppose I'm more contemplative about this stuff today because I keep finding myself weighing the merits of working outside the home . . . I am seriously considering the possibility of quitting my job."

"*What?*" Brooke and Annabeth exclaimed almost in unison. "You love that job!" added Annabeth.

"I do love working in public relations for OrganizationUSA," Andrea agreed. "But by the time I commute home at night to join the family after Chet has picked the kids up from Montessori, I don't feel like the boys are getting the best of me."

"But Andrea, I thought your company was so great for that stuff . . . isn't OrganizationUSA on the *Working Mother* Top 50 companies for working women every year?"[3] Brooke inquired.

"We sure are . . . you've probably seen the ads on TV about that, and I hope you also read the brilliant press releases written by yours truly," Andrea bragged with a smile. "But truth be told, a lot of those 'top whatever' awards are based on the work-life policies that are on paper. So we have parental leave polices—even including adoptive leave—and lots of flexible work options, including part-time work and job sharing, and a great dependent care subsidy that can be used for children or elders. But policies don't mean anything until they are put into action. I have watched people try to negotiate work-life arrangements that are more flexible, and it is less clear-cut than what is on paper."

Annabeth wondered aloud, "How can that be? If it says you can take leave or work part time, you can, right? End of story."

"At OrganizationUSA, supervisors differ in terms of how flexible they are . . . and even the really good ones sometimes send mixed messages. They'll tell us to live a 'balanced' life, but then we have so many projects to do that we end up taking work home with us. My supervisor has sent emails at 4:30 A.M. on multiple occasions . . . what kind of message about 'balance' does that send? When that is how she operates, then me asking to just work 'part time' feels weird. Not to mention that the single workers and those without children are sort of bitter about the policies, so I feel pressure from them not to use them as well," Andrea explained.

Brooke jumped on the pause in conversation. "This is a weird coincidence, because I just read an article in the *New York Times*[4] about how highly educated, professional women are leaving the workforce to stay at home and raise their children while their husbands provide for the family, at least until their kids start school—like Annabeth. The women in the article attended Ivy League schools, and most had graduate degrees . . . but the author asserted that although they should have had 'the key to the kingdom' with these credentials, they were choosing to stay at home with their children in response to the unrealistic demands of their workplaces. She said this is an indication of progress, because these women are calling out—and rejecting—the workplace and its lack of accommodation to working mothers. She actually calls it a revolution—*The Opt-Out Revolution*."

"My mom sent me a pdf of that article, too . . . but I hadn't made the connection to our conversation," confessed Annabeth. "In the email, she said something about how perhaps I wasn't just 'wasting my education after all' and how 'maybe there was still hope for me to be a feminist role model of a working mother for Joslyn, just later in life'—you know her issues with me choosing to stay at home while having earned an MBA. After giving it a read, I went to the online discussion board just to see what people were saying about it, and boy did my self-esteem plummet for a while after that. I can't believe we haven't talked about this article until now!" she said in anticipation.

Andrea wanted to know more. "Well, I haven't read it . . . so what else should I know about the article or the discussion board . . . what about it could impact your self-esteem, Annabeth?"

"Well of course I can't recite the posts word-for-word,[5] but they really empha-sized how this was not a choice that everyone was free to make. One post dis-cussed how there are no media debates and social movements over the balance of work and family for women who *have* to go to work to support their families. Others echoed how in many families, two incomes (or the income of a single mother/parent) are necessary for survival, and no 'choice' is really involved, while for other families whether women work is not about necessity but about movement from lower-middle class to middle class to upper-middle class lives.[6] Instead, it is a privileged choice to be able to have the luxury of staying at home, because you need to have a partner who has the financial means to support you. I don't disagree, but some people really went off. One person said the article was 'a feel good piece for the Muffy set to discuss while having coffee at Starbucks in their lycra gym outfits'."

Brooke recognized the irony. "Well, we're not at Starbucks, but we are drink-ing KidPlace concessions lattés. And check out our outfits!"

"Yep . . . you're reinforcing why my self-esteem took a hit because I recog-nized myself a bit in the women the articles profiled, and then on the discussion board, they were just *torn to shreds*. There was the Muffy thing . . . and then they were called pampered brats who married money . . . and "wealthy, educated ueber-moms'. . . and I remember someone saying something like 'the glorification of indulged women's choices is disturbing'."

"Wow, that's some harsh stuff . . . I only read the article so I hadn't actually thought much about how 'choice' might be an artificial term for many women," Brooke admitted.

"Wait . . . I'm not done with the online guilt trip. This one's a doozy. One per-son posted about 'loving the way this new breed of stay-at-homes are quick to point out that they are educated as if that makes them a higher line of housewife, as in I do this because I want to, not because I'm a stupid welfare mother or uned-ucated truck driver's wife.' I just kept thinking to myself, do I send off that vibe? Those words kind of haunt me . . . But one thing I read pertains *directly* to this conversation, Andrea." Annabeth continued, "One person posted a pretty smart response that really stuck with me. She said that 'when women who *can* choose to 'opt-out' take the opportunity, then issues of work and family remain individual responsibilities. If women don't push organizations or government for provisions for *everyone* in the United States who has children, the decisions become further privatized and based on race, gender, and especially socioeconomic status . . . and this precludes a larger discussion of universal health care, flex time, standard overtime pay, subsidized and good child care.' This made me feel guilty about my choice to stay at home . . . like I should be out there fighting the fight."

"Don't beat yourself up, Annabeth . . . when you had your kids, you wanted to stay home with them. And you have the means to do so . . . it doesn't mean you are a bad person!" comforted Andrea. She continued, "Well, even though I did not see the article y'all are talking about, I have been reading a book that echoes some of the themes—it's called *The Mommy Myth*[7]. The authors talk about how a 'new momism' is being offered in public discourse that poses a set of impossible ideals and redefines all women in relationship to children . . . telling us how we should be with our kids 24/7 or we're not good mothers. They were saying how the discourse is marginalizing to minority women in the United States. I didn't really quite get why before, but come to think of it, that public discourse and pressure to 'stay at home if you are able to' is really directed at women based on socioeconomic class . . . and probably race."

Brooke chimed in, "Yeah . . . you're right. We're told that staying home is the best thing for our kids, but if we were lower income women—especially an under-represented minority—we would instead be told that the best thing we can do is to get a job so that we can live independent of welfare. It really is an opposite expectation."

Annabeth said, "The woman who cleans my house has sometimes talked about her struggles and those of her extended kin. She'd like to be home more, but she has to work and has struggled to find acceptable childcare arrangements. She does have a solution at least one day a week; I have Latasha just bring her kids out with her to play with mine while she cleans."

"Well . . . I can see how all of this made you feel guilty, Annabeth," Andrea mused. "Thinking from the perspective of a different socioeconomic class does make me feel a bit indulged. Obviously, I am not working to put sustenance on the table, like Latasha. So am I working because I love it? Or am I working to provide Carter and Colton with Montessori school, swim lessons, designer clothes, and an address in the 'best' school district? In that frame, I have more choices than I usually recognize . . ."

After Andrea loaded the boys into the van to head home, she turned on a movie so she could think on the drive. "Well, this whole Opt-Out Revolution thing has given me more to think about," she thought to herself. Should she "opt out" of her job at OrganizationUSA to stay at home . . . even though she loved her job? Should she just push to use some work-life benefits available to her? Would she be letting other women down by making a private decision that precludes more public discussion of accommodations that should be made for working mothers? While she was not under a time crunch to decide, she needed some resolution to quiet her spirit.

endnotes

1. Shellenbarger, S. (2004, January 22). Undercover mom: How working women swap wardrobes, roles through the day. *Wall Street Journal, 243*(15), p. D1.
2. Medved, C. E., & Kirby, E. L. (2005). Family CEOs: A feminist analysis of corporate mothering discourses. *Management Communication Quarterly, 18,* 435–478.
3. See http://www.workingmother.com/
4. Belkin, L. (2003, October 26). The opt-out revolution. *The New York Times,* pp. 42–47, 58, 85–86.
5. The New York Times. (2003, October–November). Online bulletin board devoted to The Opt-Out Revolution. Retrieved October 1, 2004 from http://forums.nytimes.com/top/opinion/readersopinions/forums/magazine/archivedmagazinediscussions/the optoutrevolution/
6. See Crouter, A. C., & Booth, A. (Eds.) (2004). *Work-family challenges for low-income parents and their children.* Mahwah, NJ: Lawrence Erlbaum Associates.
7. Douglas, S., & Michaels, M. W. (2004). *The mommy myth: The idealization of motherhood and how it has undermined women.* New York: Free Press.

"I Feel Like I Won't Be a Good Mom if I Don't at Least *Try*"

The Breastfeeding Debate

Sherianne Shuler

KEY TERMS

- ◆"doing" gender in personal life
- ◆double bind
- ◆discrimination
- ◆generational issues
- ◆mommy guilt

"Can you believe this?" Ruby cried as she threw a magazine at her sister and flopped down on the glider on her mom's front porch.

Lucy, her 32-year-old "baby" sister, rubbed her seven-month pregnant belly as she picked up and glanced at the front cover of *Babytalk* magazine. The cover shot was a wide-eyed baby nursing. Even though the angle of the photo only showed a profile of the breast with no nipple, it *was* kind of surprising to see a boob. Not knowing exactly what Ruby was getting at, she said, "um . . . what's wrong with it?"

"There's nothing wrong with *that*, but didn't you see the article in the paper today about the controversy?" Ruby asked.

"I have no idea what you are talking about. I've been here since 8 A.M., helping mom with the girls," Lucy replied.

"Where are my sweeties, anyway?" Ruby asked, referring to her 11-month-old twin girls, whose daycare was closed today for inservice. Luckily, her mom and sister lived in town and were good backups.

Lucy answered, "They've both been napping for about 45 minutes, and mom is lying down, too. I've got the monitor right here and haven't heard a peep from their room."

"God, my boobs are about to explode! Hopefully they'll wake up soon and get me out of my misery," Ruby exclaimed. "So, anyway, apparently after this magazine came out, there was a big backlash about it, and a lot of people have been writing in and complaining that it is indecent and gross. Can you believe that? This magazine is one that only new moms get—surely they have been exposed to boobs before. This, right on the heels of that nursing mom getting kicked off the airplane because she refused to cover her baby up with a blanket."

"Yeah, that seemed unfair, but this cover is a little surprising" Lucy admitted, though she treaded carefully with her "lactivist" sister. Ruby was a dedicated breastfeeder and had been kind of preachy about it since the twins were born. Lucy knew that Ruby assumed that her baby sister would be as committed to nursing when Gavin arrived in a few months, but secretly she was not so sure about it.

"Surprising? To see a mother using her breast for its God-given purpose? No one seems to complain when they are flaunted across the cover of *Cosmo,* but this very innocent and natural photo is gross? And on that flight I'm sure there were plenty of women in revealing shirts who didn't get kicked off. It's like it's fine to show off the girls as long as they are sexualized and not being used for feeding babies," Ruby fumed. "It just pisses me off. And as a mom-to-be who will be breastfeeding in a couple of months, it should piss you off, too."

Lucy's thoughts flashed quickly to her husband. Walter had teased her the other day that "he was always bracing himself for her to turn into a crazy hormonal pregnant woman and go off on some tirade." Imagine if he had married Ruby, she smiled to herself—she can tirade whether pregnant or not. Before Lucy could answer Ruby's call to arms, the front door opened and their mom, Nellie, stepped out. "Hey, sweetie! How long have you been here? I just took a little power nap with the girls. They are both still sleeping like logs," she said, stretching as she plopped down on the glider beside her oldest daughter. Seeing the magazine cover, she visibly startled and remarked, "that's kind of . . . disturbing."

"Disturbing, Mom? Seriously?" Ruby asked.

"Honey, I know you nurse the twins and I have no problem with that. But I don't really like to see it. I mean, it's one thing when you are doing it privately, but I feel embarrassed when I see women nurse in public. It just doesn't seem very modest," Nellie explained, "like that woman on the airplane. I would feel awkward sitting next to her, and your father definitely wouldn't want to be stuck there!"

"But most women are discrete—it's not like they just whip it out and flap it around!" Ruby cried, exasperated. "Why is a mom feeding her baby even an issue? It makes no sense. Even the government is pushing breastfeeding these days; everyone knows it's best for the babies. And besides, it's legal in most states to breastfeed in public. Those flight attendants should be fired!"

"I don't know about that, but when you girls were little everyone used formula because we thought it was healthier. None of my friends even considered nursing, it was just seen as primitive," Nellie said, "and you two certainly turned out just fine. No one ever hassled me about feeding you a bottle in public. The only women I knew of who breastfed back in my day were hippies—certainly not girls like me."

Before Ruby could respond, they heard one of the girls talking over the baby monitor. "Well, I guess I'll just go inside alone and do my disgusting deed!" she huffed as she went through the front door.

Lucy turned to her mother, "do you really think breastfeeding is disgusting?"

Nellie sighed, "I know it's the natural thing to do and all, and it's becoming more accepted, but I just can't get over how strange it seems."

"I know what you mean," Lucy replied, "my doctor has given me lots of information about how much healthier it is for the baby, and they talked about it in our childbirth class. And then there's all those pro-breastfeeding posters and ads in doctor's offices and in the pregnancy magazines. Hell, even the government is putting out pro-breastfeeding ads. I feel like I won't be a good mom if I don't at least *try,* but it seems like a lot of work. All of my friends have at least tried it, but most of them have had trouble getting it to work. It's overwhelming to think that's just one more thing to learn after Gavin's born. But I certainly don't want Ruby to hear me talking this way!"

"Oh, honey, don't put that much pressure on yourself. I'm sure that whatever you decide will be fine. You know your sister, she's . . . shall we say . . . *passionate,*" her mom reassured her.

"Well, that's the understatement of the year," Lucy laughed. "Hey, tell everyone goodbye for me, will you? I need to run and meet Walter for dinner. We're trying to have as many date nights as we can before Gavin comes along!"

"Don't stress about this too much, honey," Nellie said. "You'll know what's right for you. I've been meaning to tell you that pregnancy really seems to agree with you. Back when I was carrying you girls, it was kind of embarrassing to be pregnant. You tried to hide your belly as much as possible, but now I am happy that you girls can show off your bellies a little bit. Things have changed a lot since I was pregnant, but one thing that doesn't change is that part of becoming a mother involves always second-guessing yourself or wondering if you are making the right choices. Try not to let that make you crazy!"

"Thanks, Mom," Lucy said and blew her a kiss as she walked down the porch steps.

"Love ya, honey—drive carefully and say hi to Walter for me," Nellie called out as she watched Lucy waddle to the car.

Walter was already sitting at a table at their favorite Thai restaurant when Lucy arrived. He smiled and waved when he saw his wife walk in the door. Though he had been reluctant initially, Walter was surprising Lucy with how excited he was to become a father. He had eagerly attended all Lucy's doctor appointments and childbirth classes and had also been reading up on birthing methods and new-born care. He stood and kissed his wife as he pulled out her chair.

"Hey, love, how was your day of twin-sitting at your mom's?" he asked.

"Exhausting!" Lucy replied, "I kept reminding myself that we're only going to have one, not two!"

"That's right," Walter said, "I don't know how Ruby and Andy manage with two."

"They are so sweet, though. Every time I'm around them I'm more excited to meet Gavin," Lucy added, "but next time I get the big idea to offer to help watch the girls, remind me that maybe I should rest during my days off!"

"Seriously, sweetie, you need to take your own advice. Next week maybe you should go get a massage or something on your comp day," Walter urged.

"I have something on my mind that I want to talk to you about," Lucy suddenly interjected.

"Okaaay . . ." Walter said, suddenly feeling worried that he was in trouble. Before Lucy could continue, the waiter came to take their orders. After he left, Walter looked at Lucy expectantly, "What's on your mind?"

"Ruby and Mom and I were talking about breastfeeding this afternoon. You know how strongly Ruby feels about it," Lucy began. "What do you think about it? I know some husbands don't like it."

"Um, well, I think it's obviously your body and your decision. But we've read all that stuff about how it's good for the baby and I'm all for giving Gavin the best possible start in life. I've also read about how important it is for fathers to be supportive of nursing moms and I want to be that for you, because breast-feeding obviously puts more of the burden on you," Walter answered.

"I know, and that's part of what I'm worried about," Lucy continued, "I mean, in some ways it seems like it's the feminist thing to do, to be pro-nursing, honor motherhood, yada, yada, yada. On the other hand, we could share feeding responsibilities more and going back to work would be much easier if I don't nurse. Aren't those feminist ideals, too?"

"True, but, I really think that it's better for Gavin to get breastmilk and not formula. It is supposed to build up the immune system and cut down on obesity, allergies, ear infections, and stuff like that. The American Academy of Pediatrics recommends nursing exclusively for at least a year to get the maximum benefits. And I was reading on a dad blog about how evil the formula companies are. You know those government ads that promote breastfeeding for at least six months? The formula lobby pressured the government to tone them down. And even worse, they have shamelessly marketed their products to poor women and women in third-world countries where clean water is difficult to come by. Even though breastfeeding would clearly be in the best interest of those women and babies, the big formula companies have misled them into thinking that formula is better just to make a buck. Even for us, it will be so much cheaper to breastfeed. Just one of those cans of formula is, like, $20! With needing to pay for daycare and start a college fund for Gavin, I'm thinking about how we could really use that money. But, of course, even though that's how I feel, I'm not the one with the boobs."

Lucy smiled, she could always count on Walter to figure out a way to insert both progressive politics *and* husbandly supportiveness into his opinions. "I think one of the biggest things I'm worried about is going back to work," she said, "I mean, I've heard horror stories about those breast pumps. I couldn't bring myself to list one on our baby registry—it seems too personal!"

"Do y'all have a nursing room?" Walter asked, "I just got a memo about ours this last week. HR has set up a room with couches and a TV and a fridge where nursing moms can go to pump on their breaks. Apparently companies legally have to provide a place and time to do that."

"Ha!" laughed Lucy, "there are hardly any women in my department. The last woman who tried to pump at work was Beth—a couple of years ago—and she was the butt of jokes every time she closed her office door because we all knew what she was doing in there. Now I kind of wish I hadn't laughed," Lucy admitted. "It may be a legal requirement, but that doesn't mean that the culture is supportive. Especially in the old boys club that is my office."

"Maybe you should go talk to Beth about it," Walter suggested.

"That would be a good idea, but she quit six months ago after her second baby was born," Lucy said.

"Well, can you talk to your boss, or HR? Find out what they will do to accommodate you. And maybe you can also talk to Ruby or some of your friends about how they managed," Walter suggested.

"I guess, but I just feel kind of creeped out about the whole thing. I don't want everyone at work to be thinking about my boobs. I've worked too long to be taken seriously there. I just want to have Gavin, take my eight weeks, and then go back and show everyone that I can still work as hard as they can. Ruby's a tenured professor who teaches gender courses, for God's sake! She doesn't have the same work situation in the slightest," Lucy explained.

"But you know that she'd listen and be supportive if she knew that you were unsure," Walter encouraged, "and maybe she can give you more of the positive story about nursing to help balance out your concerns. Right now maybe she just assumes you are looking forward to it because she did."

"Yeah, but she's so gung-ho about it, I'm afraid that she's going to think less of me if I don't want to do it," Lucy said, sighing, "As a feminist, I support the idea of nursing, and the right of women to do it in public. And as a health conscious person, I understand the health benefits. But it also seems like a big hassle. Would not doing it make me a bad mother, as those pro-nursing government ads imply?"

"Of course not, sweetie, you are going to be a great mother either way," reassured Walter, "I guess it really is ironic to be shaming women *into* nursing, and then shaming women *for* nursing. I hadn't really thought about it that way."

"Talk about a double-bind," sighed Lucy, "I'm damned if I do and damned if I don't. And what if I want to, but can't?"

"Honey, please try not to be too stressed about this. Gavin's coming soon, and we need to be celebrating and getting excited, not fretting over things like this," Walter said as he reached over and rubbed her shoulder. Just then, their curry and pad thai arrived. Lucy was relieved to have the chance to change the subject and to focus on eating. She did not realize how strongly pro-nursing Walter was, though he ultimately would leave the decision up to her. Everyone seems to have an opinion about breastfeeding, and she was not sure who would be most helpful to her in figuring out what she was going to do. "*Ow!*" she cried as Gavin delivered a sharp jab to her rib cage, "I guess he likes the curry!" His enthusiastic kicking only reminded her that he would be here before they knew it. Meanwhile, she had just a few more weeks to mull this over.

REPRODUCING←→CHALLENGING GENDER/ED REALITIES

introduction

The cases in this section highlight the intersection of gender/ed identity with larger social networks and systems as individuals take actions that *reproduce↔challenge gender/ed realities.* The characters in these cases are facing the decision of whether or not to reproduce gender/ed realities through silence or to resist this reproduction and instead challenge the members of their social networks through conversation.

24 "How Is *That* Going to Work?": Explaining Commuter Marriage to Others, by Karla Mason Bergen

25 "Look, Not Everybody Can Get Pregnant!": When Private Issues Are Made Public, by Jennifer J. Bute

26 "You're Totally Her Work Husband": Managing Misconceptions in the "Work-Spouse" Relationship, by M. Chad McBride and Erika L. Kirby

27 "With You We Got a Twofer": Challenging the Affirmative Action Hire Stereotype, by Brenda J. Allen

28 "Don't Be So Gay!": Challenging Homophobic Language, by Erika L. Kirby

"How Is *That* Going to Work?"

Explaining Commuter Marriage to Others

Karla Mason Bergen

KEY TERMS

- ◆ work-life "balance"
- ◆ patriarchy
- ◆ identity formation
- ◆ caregiving
- ◆ gendered roles (home)

Sarah sighed as she hung up the phone and stared out the window of her third-floor office in the Arts and Sciences building. She loved being back in college teaching, but she was sick and tired of fighting other people's ideas of what marriage was supposed to be.[1] She often thought to herself, "Isn't this the twenty-first century, for God's sake?" Her husband, Jeff, had called to report the latest hometown gossip. Earlier that morning, the pastor of their church in Plainville, had visited Jeff at his office. Jeff had built a successful accounting practice over the past 20 years while Sarah had taken primary responsibility for the home detail and raising their two now-grown children. Pastor Jerry had walked into Jeff's private office, closing the door behind him. With a somber look, he looked Jeff straight in the eye and said, "I am so sorry to hear about you and Sarah." Jeff had looked up from his work and responded with a straight face. "I'm sorry, I'm not sure what you are talking about, Jerry. What did you hear?" "Well, I understand that Sarah has moved out and is filing for divorce," said Pastor Jerry as he squirmed a little. Jeff had almost giggled and probed further. "Really. Now where did you hear that?" Jeff was not willing to let Jerry off the hook easily. Pastor Jerry confessed, "Well, a church member stopped by my office this morning. She thought that perhaps I should call on you."

Reporting this interchange to Sarah on the phone, Jeff had speculated "No doubt we were the hot topic of conversation at the coffee shop this morning."

"And so what did you tell him?" Sarah was anxious to know.

"I set him straight in a hurry," Jeff assured her. "I told him that there was no substance to the rumor. I told him that you had been hired at State University to teach math and use that master's degree that you've been wasting for 20 years. And that they were encouraging you to get your doctorate, to boot! I told him that even though it was true that you were staying in an efficiency apartment near the campus during the week, you've been coming home every weekend and things are *just fine* between us."

Sarah sighed again. She was sure the fact that they had not been to church lately because she was so tired when she was home on weekends fueled the rumors. She had no clue when she decided to take this teaching position that she and Jeff would become fodder for the town grapevine. Their kids, Bryan and Amanda, were grown and married and busy with their own careers. She had gladly supported Jeff and done what she could to make life easier for him while he worked long hours building up his practice. She had pretty much single-parented, paid the bills, run the errands, arranged their social life, and taken care of all the family obligations on both his and her side of the family, plus been heavily involved in volunteer work at their church and the children's school. But now, with the kids grown and Jeff's practice firmly established, it was *her turn!*

And Jeff agreed. He knew how much she had loved teaching at a small private college before they were married and how she had given that up to move with him to his hometown in a rural part of the state. They had discussed first her applying for, and then accepting, this position with all it entailed, including the 400-mile round-trip drive from their home. She knew that she was lucky to be offered the position with only a master's degree because these days, most college instructors had doctorates. Jeff agreed that this was a wonderful opportunity for Sarah, and they had decided together that the best solution was for Sarah to get a small apartment near campus during the week. Her salary, although modest, was the most she had ever earned and would comfortably pay her expenses during the week.

"Why are people so quick to assume that we are getting a divorce?" Sarah wondered aloud to Jeff.

"Well, I suppose it's because most married people do live together and when someone moves out, it's generally because they're not getting along," he ventured.

"But I *didn't* move out!" protested Sarah.

"Well, you know that so little happens in this town, anything out of the ordinary is grist for the rumor mill," Jeff reminded her.

"I know," sighed Sarah, "and that's why I'm glad to have something to talk about with my colleagues besides who's in the hospital, who's getting divorced, and who died. But hey, I need to be getting ready for my next class . . . I'll talk with you again this evening . . . usual time."

"Okay, but don't let this ruin your day," counseled Jeff. "I was plenty pissed off when Jerry came barging in here, but people will see that there is nothing to the rumor when you keep coming home every weekend and there is no divorce. Talk to you later."

Sarah turned back from staring out the window while recalling her conversation with Jeff. She absolutely had to get ready for her next class. But she was still puzzled why other people seemed quick to assume that her commuting three hours to take a job she wanted so much meant that she was leaving her husband. It was not that the job was more important than Jeff or her family; it was just that this was a way she could have *both*. Pastor Jerry had not been the first one to raise the idea that their marriage might be in trouble. Both she and Jeff had endured a number of questions and comments from friends and coworkers that seemed rather invasive and often designed to question the state of their marriage. Even the fairly harmless questions from other people in Jeff and Sarah's social network indicated they just did not seem to get it.

When Sarah had run into a friend one day at the grocery store and mentioned that she had been scavenging the thrift stores for her apartment near campus, Ellen had responded, "I can't believe that Jeff is actually letting you do that!" And Jeff's secretary had raised her eyebrows when Sarah had explained that she would be staying near the college during the week and inquired, "Now how is *that* going to work? What's Jeff going to do about meals? And how are you going to keep up with two places?" Their parents and children *seemed* to understand, particularly Sarah's mother, who had encouraged her from the first to pursue the opportunity to get back into college teaching. But Jeff's mother had quietly asked her one night if "things were okay between you and Jeff," and wondered if Sarah could instead find a teaching position at a nearby high school. While Jeff was bothered by such inquiries, the sexist implications of such questions really irked Sarah and she was always left feeling as though she had to defend her actions and did not know quite how to respond.

After her late-afternoon class, Sarah found herself in the elevator with Jules, a communication professor with an office on the same floor, whom she had met briefly at a faculty orientation meeting. "How's it going? Feeling like you know your way around here yet?"

"Yeah, I'm getting there," responded Sarah.

"Well, that's good. How is your husband adjusting to all of this?" Jules inquired, "Does he have supper waiting for you when you come home?"

"That would certainly be nice," Sarah admitted, "but he's two hundred miles away. I am just in town during the week to teach."

"*Oh!*" Jules exclaimed, "You have a commuter marriage! My husband and I have done that for three different periods of time, first while we were in grad school and then again after we were married. Our families thought we were nuts! But it worked for us, and it was the only way we could both finish our Ph.D.s and find jobs in our own academic areas at the same time. Thank goodness we are living together now that we have our daughter. Living apart and commuting would certainly be a challenge with a baby."

"At least I don't have that challenge to add to the mix," replied Sarah as they reached their floor and stepped off the elevator. "Both of our kids are grown and married, but Jeff has a well-established accounting practice in our hometown that he just can't up and leave. But just dealing with the perceptions of our so-called friends and neighbors back home has proved interesting. Jeff just called this morning and told me that the pastor had stopped by his office to express condolences for our impending divorce."

Jules laughed, "I know *exactly* what you mean. But there are a lot of us around. Commuting is fairly common among academics and other highly educated professionals. I've got a meeting right now, but why don't you stop in sometime? I've got a couple of books on my shelf that I think would be helpful to you."

"Thanks, I'll do that," Sarah gratefully accepted. "And perhaps you can give me some advice on how to deal with all of these idiotic questions other people are asking us about commuting. Like what my husband is doing about meals."

"I'd *love* to visit with you," assured Jules, "I can tell you stories that make the preacher story sound pretty tame."

As Sarah unlocked the door to her office, she reflected that she had not realized commuter marriages were so common. She wondered if other commuting couples had to put up with the same kinds of questions and comments from others as she and Jeff did. Did other people *always* believe that couples who lived apart because of their careers had marital problems? After settling in at her desk, she went online to research commuter marriages. Sarah googled the term "commuter marriage." "Oh my! Who would have known? 8,970 hits!" She browsed through the first two or three page of links. There were links to articles in newspapers and magazines attesting to the increasing numbers of couples in commuter marriages.

Two book titles kept coming up, one by a woman named Winfield[2] and another written by two sociologists named Gerstel and Gross[3]. Sarah found websites providing online support for couples in commuter marriages and other long-distance relationships. One website even advertised an opportunity for commuting spouses to participate in a research study being conducted at a major research university. She was particularly impressed that this website was created by a social psychologist and seemed to serve as a central distribution point for the work of academics who studied a variety of types of long-distance relationships. One article that really caught her eye was entitled, "Communicating with Your Social Network about Your Commuter Marriage." Wow! She was going to have to email Jeff a link to this website.

Sarah decided to go to the college library website and did a quick search for books on "commuter marriage." The same two titles that had popped up in her google search were there. But she noted that both of these books were from the mid-1980s. A search of the scholarly databases turned up half a dozen articles in academic journals. Sarah emailed the PDF files of the articles to her home email account to print off and share with Jeff. Maybe Jules had something more recent than those two books from the 1980s. If 3.5 million Americans were in commuter marriages, as one of the more recent newspaper articles had stated, surely there was something more current. But Sarah could not afford to spend any more time on this personal research project right now; she had a class to prep for tomorrow, a stack of student papers, and a Lean Cuisine® waiting for her at her apartment. She would make it a point to stop by Jules' office in the next few days to find out about those books.

A couple of days later, Sarah ran into Jules in the coffee room. "I've been looking for you; I wanted to take you up on that offer to look at those books on commuter marriage that you were telling me about."

"Why don't you just come down there with me now?" Jules invited. "I'll just pull them off the shelf." Coffee mugs in hand, they walked together the short distance down the hall to Jules' office. Jules walked over to a bookcase and pulled out two volumes, handing them to Sarah. "Here they are. These were really helpful for me when we started commuting."

Sarah glanced at the books. "These are the same ones I kept running across when I was doing a web search. I thought maybe there would be something more current out there."

Jules shrugged, "You know, there really isn't a ton out there on commuter marriage. Other than a handful of journal articles, I've seen a couple of popular press books on commuter marriage, but I'm not sure if they are really based on research. These two have great information that *is* based on scholarly research, even if they are a bit dated." Jules continued, "And it would just be great for you to talk to some other women who have been in commuter marriages. You've met Eva in the Spanish department? She'd be another good person for you to talk to.

Her husband's at a university in the Dominican Republic. She goes there over winter break and summers and he comes here a couple of times a year. The three of us should get together for lunch sometime."

"That would be great!" Sarah exclaimed. "I've been feeling like a scorned outsider, almost like Hester Prynne in *The Scarlet Letter,* and I now find out that there are at least two other women on my floor who've done the commuter marriage thing."

Jules replied, "That's really funny you'd say that. Winfield says in her book that women who commute *are* treated like Hester Prynne—as though they are wearing a big red 'A'—because they defy what society has deemed as the 'proper role' for women. As they say, 'women's place is in the home.' It's fine for us to have careers as long as we are home every night to make dinner and do the laundry and all the other things good wives are supposed to do. But it does seem to be beyond some people to understand that women can be 'good' wives if they pursue a career that requires commuting. My in-laws had a fit when Richard and I decided to commute again after we were married. My mother-in-law actually told me that if I wanted my marriage to work, I would stay in Boston with Richard even if there was no job for me. 'Men get lonely, Jules,' she said. 'If wives aren't there for their husbands, they have only themselves to blame if he goes looking somewhere else'."

"Oh geez . . . How do you respond to someone like that?" Sarah exclaimed.

"I didn't," Jules went on, "I wasn't going to dignify that comment with a response."

"I guess I haven't got to that point yet," Sarah reflected. "I feel like I need to justify why I'm the one who is away from home because of my job. I wonder if I'd feel the same way if I was a man?"

"Probably not," responded Jules. "Because you know that throughout history, *men* have had to often be away from home to fulfill their masculine roles, whether it was to hunt food or fight wars, engage in commerce or serve in political offices. That's seen as part of the male role and being the breadwinner. Our role as women, on the other hand, has pretty much been tied to home—keeping the home fires burning, so to speak."

"I thought we had dispelled those roles in the 1970s after the second wave of the women's movement," Sarah ventured.

"I've been reading a book on that very topic," Jules noted. "It's called *Flux*[4] by Peggy Orenstein, and it talks about how our society is sort of 'in between' figuring out women's roles. While in many ways, women are encouraged to pursue professional paths that were not open to women even 30 or 40 years ago, they are often still judged in the old ways that tend to associate women with care taking."

"Well, that makes a lot of sense and totally fits with what I've been experiencing. But that doesn't really help me decide how to respond to other people who ask questions or make comments about our marital arrangement. It seems like I'm always caught off-guard when someone asks one of those ridiculous questions or makes a comment hinting that Jeff and I are doing this because we don't get along. Do I really have to give everyone a whole long explanation? Or do I even respond?" Sarah wondered.

"I guess that's up to you," responded Jules. "Me, I always figured it was none of anyone else's business. How my husband and I agree to conduct our marriage is up to us. But I do sort of understand that feeling of compulsion to set people straight. You'll figure it out."

As Sarah walked back to her office, books in hand, she thought about leaving later in the day to head "home" for the weekend. She and Jeff had decided that it was time to make an appearance in church on Sunday, but she dreaded facing the predictable questions and comments from others. How would she deal with them? Was it possible to maintain a good marriage and a highly demanding job in spite of what other people thought?

endnotes

1. This case is based on the author's dissertation, *Women's Narratives about Commuter Marriage: How Women in Commuter Marriages Account For and Negotiate Identities with Members of their Social Networks.* The author wishes to thank the American Association of University Women for the American Fellowship than enabled her to conduct this original research study for her dissertation.
2. Winfield, F. E. (1985). *Commuter marriage: living together, apart.* New York: Columbia University Press.
3. Gerstel, N., & Gross, H. (1984). *Commuter marriage: A study of work and family.* New York: Guildford Press
4. Orenstein, P. (2000). *Flux: Women on sex, work, kids, love, and life in a half-changed world.* New York: Doubleday.

"Look, Not Everybody Can Get Pregnant!"

When Private Issues Are Made Public

Jennifer J. Bute

KEY TERMS

- ◆ sexual and reproductive health
- ◆ gendered roles in the home
- ◆ sexism

Anna sat down at her desk, opened her Internet browser, and clicked on her favorite news website. She liked to start her days at the office slowly—sipping coffee and scanning the latest headlines. On this particular morning, a headline addressing a very personal issue caught her eye: "Are You on the Quest for a Baby? Join Our Readers Live as They Debate the Ideal Age for Baby-Making." Anna's heart raced as she clicked the link to the chat room.

She was, indeed, on the "quest" for a baby. She and her husband, Brad, had been trying to get pregnant for almost two years. As she approached the magic age of 35, Anna was becoming more and more anxious about her ability to have a child. She had consulted books, websites, and fertility specialists, and most seemed to suggest that her chances of getting pregnant declined steeply after turning 35. As she read the reader comments on the "ideal" age to have a baby, Anna found herself getting angry. "Women should have babies when they're young and energetic!" wrote Annette from Georgia. "Ladies, get off the career track and on the baby track before you regret it," said Jill from New York. "Having babies at the age of 40 is just wrong," said Cathy from Indiana. Anna finally closed the web page in frustration and left her office to take a short walk.

Even though she had heard comments like these before, they bothered her more than usual today. She and Brad had married when they were both 30 and started trying to have a family after two years of marriage. Now quickly approaching 35, Anna wondered, "Should we have started trying even sooner?" But they had wanted time together before adding a baby to the mix. They had travelled during their first year of marriage, bought and restored an old home, adopted two dogs from a local shelter, embarked on exciting careers, and then settled down to have a family. "I thought that's what newlyweds were supposed to do, but lately I've found myself regretting these delays. What if we had tried to have a baby right after we got married?" she wondered. Now after a series of fertility treatments, including an array of invasive tests and hormone shots, Anna felt no closer to having a child.

At the same time, she resented the judgments implied by comments like those in the chat room. She grumbled to herself, "Why do people always assume that women, but not men, delay childbearing by putting their careers first? Don't men do this, too?" And some articles Anna had read suggested that just like women, men's fertility declines with age "so both members of a couple are responsible, right?" she thought. The people who had posted messages in the chat room certainly did not think so. Even though she and Brad made a mutual decision to wait to try for kids, people always assumed the decision was hers alone and that her advancing age mattered more than his.

And people did not hesitate to ask very personal questions about having children. When they were first married, questions like, "So, when are you going to have kids?" did not bother Anna much. She usually responded with a frank answer like, "Once we get settled, we'll start a family." But recently, since they had struggled to get pregnant, Anna felt more and more offended by these questions. One coworker who was clueless about Anna's struggles regularly asked her if she was pregnant yet. "What a personal question to ask someone you hardly know!" she fumed. She and Brad had decided to keep their fertility problems a private matter, but lately Anna found it tempting to teach nosey people a lesson by shocking them with a sarcastic answer like, "Look, not everybody can get pregnant!"

As she finished her walk, Anna found herself feeling worse, not better, but she had to get back to work. She returned to her desk and opened her email. She noticed a message from her college roommate, Lindsey. "Good news," wrote Lindsey, "Jesse and I will be adding a little one to our family in about six months. You and Brad had better get busy!" This was the last straw . . .

Anna took a deep breath and typed her reply: "Lindsey, Brad and I have been trying to get pregnant for two years. I've been giving myself shots in the stomach every day for the past six months—not everyone is as lucky as you are!" But as she poised her finger over the mouse, ready to hit "send," Anna hesitated. Was this really about Lindsey? Were the consequences of this email worth the benefits? What would really make her feel better in this situation?

"You're Totally Her Work Husband"

Managing Misconceptions in the "Work-Spouse" Relationship

M. Chad McBride and Erika L. Kirby

Chuck shut the door to his office, started up his computer, and read over the new job offer again. Two weeks ago he had been approached by Tyrone, the supervisor of a different department at Corp, about transferring from his current team to Tyrone's department. He loved the team he worked with and his responsibilities there, and he could never have imagined in such a short time that he might actually consider transferring. However, over the past few weeks, Chuck's day-to-day life had changed substantially; he reflected back on when things started to go downhill.

He had walked into the break room and was chatting with Jane, one of the newer employees on the team. "Hey Chuck—how's the new project coming along?" Jane inquired.

"Oh you know . . . it's going. We're a couple of days behind where I wanted to be, which is going to end up costing us more money in the end as well, but it'll all get done and be fine," Chuck answered.

"Uh oh . . . behind schedule *and* over budget . . . what's your wife going to think about that?"

"What are you talking about? I don't have a wife, remember?" asked Chuck.

Jane smirked: "Duh . . . I mean Melissa—she's not going to be too happy if it's late."

133

"Melissa's married, Jane. And she's our supervisor. Why did you call her my wife?" Chuck wondered aloud, obviously confused.

"Because, she's your *work wife* . . . you know, the person at work that's like your wife, but at work," explained Jane. "Julie and I were reading an article about work spouses—it's a new term for the person in the office you have a great connection to and spend most of your time with. We started talking about if we had any in our office. Of course, you and Melissa are the first people we thought of. You're totally her work husband."

"I'm not sure I like that label. What would her real husband think?" questioned Chuck.

"Well, y'all always seem to be so in sync and you always have all of those inside jokes the rest of us never get."

"Yeah . . . ever since I started working here we've totally hit it off, but we are just close friends. And she's our supervisor now . . . I don't think it's very smart to call us that. What will everyone think?" asked Chuck.

"Chuck, I'm the new one, and as I understand it, everyone has been thinking this for years behind your back. That's one of the first things I heard about when I started working here—how close the two of you were and how you had this special relationship. They just didn't have a word for it, but now we do," smiled Jane.

"Well, I don't like it. How about you keep that term on the down low?" suggested Chuck.

Of course, as was usual in their office, word spread fast, and before he knew it he was getting made fun of by nearly everyone. Although he and Melissa typically talked about everything, he found himself avoiding bringing it up to her. Even though they had their usual phone conversations during the commute home from work to get closure for the day, he still did not ask her about it . . . he secretly hoped she had not heard their new nicknames.

But a couple of days later when they were at lunch, she brought it up. "We haven't talked about it, but I guess you've heard what the office is calling us now?" Melissa asked chuckling.

"Yeah. I actually felt strange talking about it—like giving it a voice would make it real or something and make things different between us. I just really don't like that term 'work spouse.' I asked Jane to keep quiet about it, but you know how word spreads. I mean, obviously we have a great connection, but to me the tie to the marital relationship insinuates there's something improper going on—especially now that we have a different power relationship." Chuck and Melissa had hit it off soon after he started with Corp five years ago, and things had not really changed when she became the team lead seven months ago.

"Oh come on, Chuck. What can it really hurt—they're just having a little fun," said Melissa.

"I think it can hurt a lot. What about when it comes time for annual reviews? If ever I get any sort of promotion or anything, they're going to assume its because I'm your 'work husband.' "

"Well, they could have assumed that anyway—everyone knows we've been friends for as long as you've worked here. We know we're not doing anything wrong, and obviously I would not do any special favors for you or anything. We've always been above board with everything. It's just a word—who cares?"

"Well, what about your husband? Have you told him about it? I mean, James knows we're close friends. He doesn't seem to have a problem with that, but what will he think if he hears that people are calling me your husband during the day? That seems to be even more threatening than us just being friends," Chuck suggested.

"Chuck—of course he's fine with you and our relationship. I mean, we have you over to watch football on Sundays, and you've babysat our kids I don't know how many times when we needed you. He's cool with you . . ." Melissa paused, "But I do have to say I haven't told him about this newest development. I'm not sure why, but I guess it's a little weird to tell your husband that your coworkers are calling someone else your work husband," she laughed.

"See, that's what I'm talking about . . . you're with me . . . it is a little weird," said Chuck. "Do *you* think the term applies to us?"

"Well, you're the person I go to when I need something or someone. Like last year when Mom got diagnosed with cancer, I was stuck here at the office and I totally leaned on you."

"Well, of course . . . that's what friends do. And James was . . ."

". . . out of town . . . right," Melissa finished. "See, and we finish each other's sentences. I guess that's what normally happens with real spouses so I can see how someone might call us that."

"It still makes me uncomfortable. Why do we need a word for it anyway?" Chuck was still not convinced it was only harmless fun.

After lunch that day, Chuck could not stop thinking about what might happen at the company holiday party that was coming up. How would James react if someone started in on all of the work husband jokes? "If I was James, I must admit I'd feel a bit threatened," he thought. Maybe he should tell Melissa to say something to him before the party. Of course if she did, James might think it really is a big deal and then act all weird around him. As he pondered which option would be worse, he decided to google the term to see what popped up—surely he was not the only person having this experience. As he perused through the links, several articles mentioned a vault.com survey that found almost a third of people reported having a work spouse.[1] There were also several lists of tips on how to maintain a successful office marriage, including keeping doors open, always accepting phone calls from your real spouse, and minimizing physical contact. They had never talked about it, but all of these were things that he and Melissa had always done.[2] Of course they were close, but they were also professionals. Also on the list was to demystify the relationship at the office. He guessed they could try to do even more of that. Just as he was trying to figure out what "demystifying" might entail, he heard a knock at the door.

"Come in," Chuck said and looked up to see Allen leaning in the doorway.

"Hey Chuck, what's up? You look like you're upset about something."

"I'm okay . . . just sick of this work spouse crap. People need to get a life," said Chuck.

"Well, you bring it on yourself. You and Melissa spend all that time together. And remember a few months ago when y'all went on that business trip together and stayed in the same room?"

"Allen, what are you suggesting? You know how upper-management has been trying to get us to trim expenses—we were just trying to save them some money. We had separate beds—nothing happened. How many times do I have to tell people we're just friends?"

"Well, we all see the connection you two have. You can't tell me you've never thought about what it would be like if you were more than friends," said Allen.

"No, actually I haven't. She's married, Allen. We're close friends—that's it. Why is it that if a man and woman are friends, people assume one of them must want to hook up. You and I sometimes play golf, and we've stayed together on a trip before—no one's suggesting that I want to sleep with you," pushed Chuck.

"You know that's not the same. First of all, we're guys. And second, you know you and Melissa spend way more time together than we do. Who's the first person you call when something happens at work? Melissa, right? We all see it," Allen reminded him.

"Well sure, but that does not mean that either one of us wants to have sex . . ."

"What if she wasn't married. Then you probably would, huh?" interrupted Allen.

"Allen—seriously, *stop* it. I do not want to sleep with Melissa. I don't want to be married to her. She's my friend *and* my boss," said Chuck, getting more and more upset.

"Well, whatever. We'll see how big of a merit raise you get this year . . ." laughed Allen as he walked away.

Chuck sat silently fuming. "This situation is really getting out of control . . . but what can I do about it?" he wondered to himself. He thought he was trying to demystify the relationship with Allen, but the conversation did not quite go as planned. Allen laughed when he commented about the raise, but what if there was a little bit of truth in his joking? "I have not spent the last five years working my butt off to move up in the company to not be taken seriously on my own merits," thought Chuck.

The next day, as he pulled into the parking lot, Jane pulled in beside him. As they both shuffled in through the snow, Jane joked, "You better get in there and get your work wife some hot chocolate. I know you know exactly how she likes it made."

"Jane, shut it. This whole mess is your fault. If you and Julie had never read that damn article, none of this would be happening."

"You know I do it just to get a rise out of you . . . people did it before, just behind your back," Jane said. "We're all just joking around, giving you a hard time."

"Yeah, but it raises suspicion and soon enough people will really start thinking there's something going on. And how am I supposed to have any sort of credibility around here?" asked Chuck.

"Actually, there are a few people who are starting to really get upset about it," Jane confessed.

"*See* . . . you can't joke about things forever without ramifications. Who's upset?"

"Well, you know that Roy has always complained about office cliques, and he sees you two as the ringleaders with your inside jokes and your knowing glances . . . all of this is just adding fuel to his fire."

"Great . . . that's just what I need. I've worked hard to make him feel included but I guess I get to start all over with him now."

"And then there's Kelsa. You know she's had a crush on you since she started working here. When we were at lunch yesterday, she got real quiet when we were talking about it," Jane said.

"Oh God . . . what happened?" Chuck asked with trepidation.

"When we got her to finally talk, she just said, 'I always thought *I* was his work wife . . . he's closer to me than he is to Melissa anyway,'" said Jane.

"Are you kidding me? Now it's a damn competition?" Chuck cried in disbelief.

"It was hilarious, Chuck. We told her that maybe you were a work spouse polygamist and she was wife number two," laughed Jane. "Of course, she didn't like that either—she wants to be your first work wife. She's not totally stable anyway."

"That's just the problem. This really has gotten out of control. And you know how Kelsa gets when she starts drinking. We have the holiday party next week. What if she drinks too much and gets loose lips? You know James, Melissa's husband, is going to be there. If he realizes that Kelsa's jealous, he may start thinking there's actually reason for him to be concerned too."

After he made it to the office, he pulled Tyrone's email back up. When he first got the transfer offer, he was not really interested in the lateral move. Sure, there was a little bit more responsibility, but there was not really any pay increase. He loved his current position, and knew there would be some openings in his department for real upward movement. Plus he had to admit that the thought of not working with Melissa on a daily basis was a real negative. Of course, everything had changed since the office rumor mill had started up full tilt. Now, he had people actually asking him if he would have an affair with Melissa. If and when he did get to move up in the company, would he even be taken seriously or would everyone assume he had slept his way up? And to top it all off, he had a jealous coworker who wanted to claim him for her own. Kelsa was just crazy enough to really make things worse—she was known for saying inappropriate things in all sorts of settings.

He had initially just tried to ignore the talk, like Melissa suggested. When that did not work, he repeatedly denied the rumors and asked people to stop it, but nothing seemed to work. Why were people even using language from private life like "husband and wife" in the workplace anyway? And why did no one think a man and woman who were close could not just be friends? He really did not want to make the lateral transfer, but maybe it was just too much work to keep correcting everyone. Maybe he should just give up and take Tyrone's offer. He knew Tyrone wanted an answer in the next day or two . . . he'd have to make up his mind soon.

endnotes

1. Erwin, P. (2008, September 12). *7 signs you have a work spouse*. Retrieved September 15, 2008 from http://jobs.aol.com/article/_a/7-signs-you-have-a-work-spouse/200809 12151309990006

2. Jackson, K. M. (2005, October 23). *It's a marriage of sorts* (online version). Retrieved September 15, 2008 from http://www.boston.com/jobs/globe/articles/102305_spouse work.html

"With You We Got a Twofer"

Challenging the Affirmative Action Hire Stereotype

Brenda J. Allen

KEY TERMS

- ◆ stereotypes
- ◆ patriarchy
- ◆ discrimination
- ◆ gendered roles in the workplace

Kendra smiled when she saw the header "Party Time!" on an email from her team leader, Joe. He was an enthusiastic leader of their sales team in the tech division, and she knew her sales had contributed to the celebratory environment. When she was hired by the general sales manager, Ted, just a few weeks ago, he acknowledged that she would help to diversify their group—she was one of only two women and the only African-American in the tech sales division of their company. However, he had also reinforced how excited he was to have someone with her strengths and expertise in the job.

So it had taken her by surprise when one day after lunch, the other female tech salesperson, Jana, asked, "Did you hear that Joe has been referring to you as a 'twofer?'"

"What the heck does that mean?" asked Kendra.

"Well, he said it was because Ted could count you in two categories of diversity—both female and African-American," said Jana. "You know, the other person they brought in to interview for your job in tech sales was one of Joe's old college buddies. I'm sure he was disappointed he didn't have another good ole boy working in this place. Me personally, I'm glad you're here. I can't believe it took five years for them to hire another woman."

Kendra had decided not to let Jana's comments about Joe bother her. Since Ted had seemed to try to assure her that she was hired for her qualifications, she had chosen to just let her actions speak and demonstrate that she was actually more than qualified to do her job. So far, she had done quite well. She had contributed quite a bit to the team already, including making a significant contribution to the increased sales this month.

Coming back from her recollections to the email, she noticed Joe had addressed the email to all team members: "Good job this month, everyone. We exceeded our quota by 22 percent!!! Let's celebrate by having a little party in the conference room this Friday afternoon. Kendra, would you organize everything? You can use the corporate credit card to buy some snacks and whatever else you think we'll need. Let's party hearty, everybody!"

Kendra felt her heart racing. While she had significant sales this month, Joe had not recognized her efforts in the email. Of course, everyone had some sales in the past month as well, and she did not want to be perceived as glory-hungry, especially in the first month. But she wondered, "Was Joe threatened by my productivity this month? And why does he want me to arrange the party?" Kendra mused. "Did he assume I'm good at planning social events because I'm a woman, or more specifically, because I'm a black woman?" She did not think she had done anything to give him or anyone else the impression that she was good at planning social events. Or, was there another explanation? Is this part of where the "twofer" comment came from? Especially if he was upset that his buddy did not get hired and thought of her as an "Affirmative Action hire," he may still be resentful toward her.

Maybe Joe singled her out because she was the newest employee? She realized she could analyze the situation all she wanted, but that would not help her decide what to do. She considered talking with Jana about it to see if she had ever experienced anything like it, but hesitated. "I want to be a team player," she thought. "I don't want my coworkers to think I'm a complaining black person, or a sassy black woman—those are all stereotypes I want to avoid. At the same time, I don't want to set a precedent of being the team's party organizer." The party was coming up and she had to decide what to do.

"Don't Be So Gay!"
Challenging Homophobic Language

Erika L. Kirby

Kira walked home from school and pondered what had happened that day. It was the third week of high school, and she was a first-year student who wanted to fit in and make a good impression. "How are people going to treat me after what happened with Tristan today? Have I already blown my chances to be popular by speaking up?" she wondered.

Exchanging books at her locker between classes, she had overheard Dylan tell Tristan that he was sore from last night's football practice. She was horrified when Tristan had replied, "Dude, man-up. We're all sore, but we don't complain about it. Don't be such a fag."

To her own surprise, she immediately responded, "Do you even know what that word means, Tristan?"

He had said, "Sure, it means Dylan is acting like a total gaywad."

Kira had been lectured from an early age on the origins of this word by her parents. "It's a bit more complex than that. Fag derives from faggot, which is a word you probably shouldn't just throw around because some people say the origins of faggot trace back to homosexual men being tied together in a bundle, or faggot, and being burned at the stake. Even if it isn't the only meaning, many people know that history of the word, and I know most people in the gay community don't appreciate hearing that word."

Tristan replied, "Well excuse me! I was just making a joke, and it's too bad you don't have a sense of humor. I'll make sure just to say he is gay from now on. Why do you care anyway? I sure hope a hottie like you isn't playing for the other team."

Kira did not know if his comment was worth following up on. Of course, just substituting gay was not any better. He would still be using "gay" as an insult to Dylan and, in turn, suggesting all gay men were whiny and weak. And she did not want to seem defensive about not being a lesbian because that might make it look like she thought being lesbian was a bad thing. She chose her next words carefully: "Even though I'm straight, Tristan, I don't have any problem with people who aren't. I just think people need to think through how words can hurt others. How do you know that a gay or lesbian person wasn't around just now? Not everyone who is GLBT[1] (gay-lesbian-bisexual-transgender) is 'out,' and you may have just reinforced for them that school is not a safe space."

Obviously more sensitive to the issue, Kira put a tally in her planner every time she heard "gay," "homo," "lesbo," "fag," or "dyke" that day, but she gave up and stopped when her tally hit 15 times. "Why can't people understand that what we say matters?" Kira wondered. She remembered how she had been socialized into understanding what it meant to be GLBT. From grade school on, her parents had never sheltered her from issues of sexual orientation—just the opposite. They explained that sometimes girls like boys (and vice versa), but that sometimes girls like girls, and sometimes boys like boys, and that we should just be happy for people when they find someone to love—no matter what. Mom had never placed on Kira the assumption that she would like boys; she would always say, "Well, someday you'll decide if you like girls or boys more, and I will love you either way."

Even when Kira herself proclaimed that she had decided she was straight and liked boys, Mom still said, "Well, until your younger brother decides the same thing, I'll still talk about liking girls or boys, okay?" Given her own socialization to be open and respectful of multiple sexual orientations, Kira did not understand why people could then use words like "gay" to intentionally (or even unintentionally) put down others.

While she had taken a stand today, she was not sure that she would be positively labeled as an "ally." People might instead label her more negatively—as a high strung bitch who cannot take a joke. Was joking that big of a deal? And correcting people was going to be hard work—she would need to speak up more than 15 times a day at the current pace! She wondered if it was even worth the potential consequences to correct people on their homophobic language. Could she make any difference if it happened that frequently?

endnote

1. GLBT (also LGBT): either of these expressions are acronyms for individuals who are gay, lesbian, bisexual, or transgender/transsexual. The acronym differs across organizations; for example, the Human Rights Campaign (HRC) utilizes GLBT while the Gay, Lesbian and Straight Education Network (GLSEN) utilizes LGBT.

(RE)POSITIONING GENDER/ED REALITIES

introduction

The cases in this section *(re)position gender/ed realities* as the main characters reflect on how to position (and reposition) themselves or the organizations of which they are a part within a particular gender/ed context. This positioning may be a gendered identity they want to move toward (e.g., OSCLG and the YWCA as feminist organizations) or move away from (e.g., a parent who re-inscribes gendered roles through toys).

29 "I Never Hit Her": Abuse between Intimates, by Julia T. Wood

30 "Like the Marines, Do We Need a Few Good Men?": Contesting the Single-Sex Mandate of the YWCA, by Lynn M. Harter, Erika L. Kirby, and Margaret M. Quinlan

31 "Our ~~Father~~ Creator Who Art in Heaven . . .": Negotiating Patriarchy in Religion and Feminism, by Erika L. Kirby

32 "If a Boy Is Playing with It, It's a Boy Toy; If a Girl Is Playing with It, It's a Girl Toy": Questioning the Gendering of Toys, by Paaige K. Turner

33 "Let Me Work the Kinks Out of Your Neck": The Story of Jared and Chris, by Diana K. Ivy and Shawn T. Wahl

34 Making Ourselves a(t) Home in Academia: The "Creatively Welcoming" Space of OSCLG, by Cynthia Berryman-Fink, Cheris Kramarae, Bobby Patton, Anita Taylor, and Virginia E. Wheeless

"I Never Hit Her"

Abuse between Intimates

Julia T. Wood

29

KEY TERMS

- ◆ gendered roles (breadwinner and homemaker)
- ◆ abuse and the cycle of violence
- ◆ division of household labor
- ◆ masculinity

"I never hit her," Jake insisted, trying not to shout. "I'm not one of those abusive men you hear about."

"Hitting a person isn't the only kind of abuse," Mike responded. "When you yell at Sandy and throw things and shove her, that's abuse."

"By that standard, raising my voice could be 'abuse,'" Jake snarled sarcastically. Mike nodded. "It could be."

Jake rolled his eyes, exasperated by these men whom he had considered allies until Sandy made him move out two weeks ago. Before that fateful night, he and Sandy were part of a group of five couples who had become close friends. Ed and Eileen, Mike and Shelly, Nick and Megan, Mark and Rita, and Jake and Sandy had met when they found themselves in the same Bible study class at their church. They were all in their mid- to late-thirties, middle class, and committed to their faith, so they had quickly bonded as a group and got together often. When Sandy threw him out, the men in the couples had decided to become his support group, meeting for an hour twice each week. Yet sometimes in these meetings Jake felt more defensive than supported—a feeling that was intensified since Ed was a family therapist by trade.

"Look, guys, get real," Jake implored. "Can any of you honestly say you've never raised your voice to your wife, never thrown anything, never lost your temper?"

147

"I'll admit that I had to leave the house once because I was so angry," offered Mike. "I thought if I stayed in the house with Shelly, I might say things I couldn't take back so I took a walk—a very long walk."

Nodding in agreement, Nick said, "Yeah, I've gotten angry with Megan, but I haven't yelled at her or shoved her. I couldn't do that to her—she's my best friend and the mother of my children."

"Rita can make me nuts at times," added Mark. "But we don't yell or break things, and I would never use my hands against her."

"Wait a minute. We're getting off track," redirected Ed. "We're talking about Jake and Sandy, not the rest of us. This isn't about Mike or Nick or Mark or me. It's about you, Jake. We're meeting because you and Sandy are going through a rough time, and we want to support you, so let's get back to you."

"If you want to support me, then why don't you acknowledge what I'm saying—that I'm not an abuser?" Jake asked. "You guys know me. You know I'm not a monster."

"You don't have to be a monster to engage in abuse," Mark said gently.

"You and Sandy have been married for 13 years. Why do you think she asked you to leave home?" asked Mike.

"I'll tell you exactly why. Ever since she got that job, she thinks she doesn't need me. She thinks she's Ms. Independent Woman, and I'm just superfluous; that's why."

"Sounds like you're angry that she went back to work," observed Ed.

"Please stop with your therapy talk," snarled Jake. "I'm not one of your clients."

Ed chuckled softly. "Just your bad luck to have a friend who is a therapist specializing in domestic violence." Looking at Jake, he continued, "But my job means that I might understand some of what you're struggling with. For instance, in my practice, I see a lot of men who are angry with their wives for taking jobs and not needing them in the same ways. It's not unusual—you're not the only man who's ever resented it when his wife became more independent."

"Everything was fine between us until she got that job and then the promotion," Jake grumbled. "She took care of the home and kids, and I took care of earning a living for the family. We each did what we were supposed to, and everything worked fine, just fine."

Jake recalled how life with Sandy used to be. Every morning, she would have a nice breakfast—not cold cereal or microwave muffins, but eggs and bacon and toast or homemade waffles—ready for him right at 7:30 so he could eat and read the newspaper before leaving at 8:00 for the office. When he got home at six each night, she had prepared a good dinner. She hadn't fixed breakfast for him since she got the promotion at the bank, and she never made great dinners anymore. Sometimes she wasn't even there when he got home at 6:00. Since she had started working, he felt unnecessary—like she didn't need him or even notice him at all.

"Well, naturally a change like Sandy's working is going to mean other changes have to happen," said Mark. "What have you done to support what she's doing?"

"What do you mean, 'support her'? I *don't* support her working. I've told her that. I make enough for both of us, and our family was fine when she stayed home." Jake huffed.

"Apparently it wasn't fine for Sandy or she wouldn't have wanted to start working," observed Mike. "Maybe she's working for reasons other than money. Maybe she likes the sense of accomplishment, just like you and I do."

"She can accomplish plenty in our home. She's a great cook—when she takes the time, which is not lately. She used to keep the house looking really nice— that's an accomplishment. Now it's never really clean anymore. Clothes don't get washed and ironed like they need to be." Jake fumed, remembering something that had really set him off. "The day of our big argument, I didn't even have a pressed shirt to wear. Can you believe that? How am I supposed to do my job when she doesn't have my clothes ready?"

"Did you ever consider ironing your own shirts?" asked Mike.

"That's not my job," Jake protested.

"Maybe your job is changing, just like Sandy's is," suggested Ed. "Marriages don't stay the same. People change, and the marriages they are in either change with them or end. Jake, you have to decide if you want your marriage to continue."

"Who are you to tell me what I have to decide?" Jake demanded.

"Who I am is a friend who cares about you," Ed replied. "I'm also a therapist who sees a lot of men who are going through what you are. In fact, I'll bet that I can tell you what happened after she took the job."

"Okay, Mr. Smart Therapist, you're on. What happened?" Jake accepted the dare.

"For a while you just didn't like it, but kept it to yourself. After a while, you felt like tension was building in you from keeping it bottled up inside and you finally exploded at Sandy—maybe that's when you yelled or broke the vase." Watching Jake, Ed knew he was batting 1,000 on describing what Jake felt. Ed was not surprised—he was merely describing the cycle of violence that is so typical in intimate violence. "After you exploded, you apologized to Sandy and for a while you were especially nice—maybe getting her flowers or something like that."

Jake stared in mild disbelief at Ed, thinking it was uncanny that Ed could know the details of what had happened between him and Sandy. When she first took the job, it was just part time, and she had said she could do it and still take care of the home. After a couple of months, she was offered a promotion to a full-time position, and she took it—without even asking him. She had come home one day and just announced it. She had acted surprised when he was not happy, but why would he be? After that, everything had gone straight downhill at home. Now she was working 50 hours a week, sometimes more, and she did not have the time to fix good breakfasts and dinners or clean the house like she used to do.

About a month after the promotion, Jake told her he wanted her to quit her job because it was hurting their family. Sandy said he could pitch in or they could hire help, but that she liked her job and was keeping it. That was the first night that he had lashed out and yelled at her. She had asked him, "Jake, calm down and be reasonable. Can't we work together on this?" For some reason, that only made him angrier, and that was when he had taken the vase that had belonged to her mother and hurled it at the wall beside her. He had not hit her (and had not meant to), but he did hurt her. He knew what that vase meant to her, and he felt bad as soon as he broke it. He had apologized and had even brought her a dozen roses the next day. How could Ed have known that?

Since that night, there had been more incidents, more yelling, more throwing. Once he grabbed her and held her down when she tried to leave the table. He wasn't through talking—and was not about to let her leave until he was. It was after the last incident that she had asked him to move out. He had been trying to reason with her about why she should quit the job, to which she had the gall to reply, "Jake, I love working and am not quitting my job at the bank." ("She used to love *me*," he'd thought at the time!) But then she said something that really infuriated him—he still could hear her words. "And if you don't start supporting my decision to work instead of making it harder on me, we might need to separate." In their 13 years of marriage, Sandy had never threatened him, and she had never suggested she would even think about betraying her marriage vows. He had shoved her into a wall and yelled at her. He could not remember exactly what he had said, but it was something about her needing to remember that he was the man in the family and that, as a woman, her role was to support him. When he finally released her, she had walked to the other room and told him to leave or she would call 911.

Jake shook his head, trying to clear the memory of that ugly night. He would have never thought he could lay a hand on Sandy. But then, he would never have thought his own wife—sweet Sandy who used to live to please him—would stop being the woman he fell in love with and married. And now he was living in a hotel and meeting with these men who said they wanted to help him but seemed to be on Sandy's side.

"I relate to how you feel, you know. I lived through the same thing with Megan," Nick said, pulling Jake back from his memories. "You might not remember, but about four years ago when our youngest entered high school, Megan started taking classes to earn her realtor's license, and she's been selling houses ever since. We had to make a lot of adjustments to make the family work once she did that."

"Like what?" asked Jake.

"Like I cook meals most nights. I use part of my weekend doing household chores that she used to do, and I do most of the chauffeuring of the kids because Megan's schedule is so erratic."

"You must resent having to do all of that." Jake said, shaking his head in disbelief.

"No. Well, not anymore, but at first I did," admitted Nick. "It took some getting used to, especially when she started earning more than I do. I had to really work to get my head around that!"

"She earns more than you?" Jake repeated. "I can't imagine that."

"It surely set my head spinning for a while. I had to work it through for a long time before I was comfortable with it. I had to ask who I am if she doesn't need me to provide for her." Nick confessed.

"It's hard to be a Prince Charming when the damsel isn't in distress and doesn't need rescuing," Ed chimed in. "How did you and Megan work things through?"

"We talked and talked and then talked some more," Nick explained. "We had to renegotiate our marriage from the ground up with a whole new set of roles."

"But I don't want new roles," Jake protested.

"I know that," Ed sympathized. "But your choice may be whether to divorce or work out new roles. Whatever you do, you're going to have to learn how to do it without violence."

"I never hit her. I'm not an abuser," Jake asserted, reprising his original defense.

"No more excuses," Mike said firmly. "You did yell. You did break things that mattered to her. You did hold her down. You did shove her. Those are acts of abuse."

"Don't tell me I'm an abuser when I know I'm not," Jake growled.

"Jake, we're here to support you, but we can't do the work for you. You have to decide to sign on or not. What's it going to be?" Nick demanded.

"Do you want me to admit I'm something I'm not? Do you want me to say I think it's great that Sandy cares more about her job than her family?" Jake asked. "I won't do that."

"Nobody's asking you to, Jake," offered Ed. "We're asking you to acknowledge that you have been violent toward Sandy—not lethally violent, not beating her, but violent anyway. You've been using your voice and your hands as weapons to control her."

"I understand that I've hurt her, but I haven't done the kind of things that a batterer would do."

Ed decided to build on Jake's first acknowledgement. He prodded, "I know I'm going to sound a bit like a therapist—it's an occupational hazard for me—but I have to tell you that what you are saying is what I hear from nearly every man I counsel."

"What do you mean?" Jake asked.

"I mean the denial—the claims that you may hurt Sandy, but that you're not really violent; that you may hold her down or push her, but that it is not 'real' violence. You are distancing yourself from what you don't want to be—an abuser." Ed watched, seeing that Jake finally seemed to be listening. "And it doesn't work, Jake. Once you start down the path of trying to control, you are not any different from anyone else on that path."

"You don't think shoving is different than battering?" Jake demanded.

"Yes and no," Ed replied. "Shoving today often becomes battering tomorrow. One of the things about violence is that it usually escalates if the people involved don't find a way to stop it. If you look at what has happened, you'll see that your anger and violence aren't staying at the same level. They are growing—each incident you've told us about was more violent than the one before it. It's going to keep going like that if you don't decide to change. If you and Sandy don't find a way to change your marriage or end it, you're likely to be more violent; you're likely to do things that are not part of the man you want to be."

After several moments of silence, Mike asked, "What's it going to be, Jake? Will you sign on to work through your issues? Or not?"

Jake sat in silence as multiple questions swam through his head. "Can these men be my friends if they think I abused Sandy? Is what I did really abuse? Do I have to label myself as an abuser to work on my marriage? Don't men have a right to exert some control over their families? Do I even want to be married to Sandy if it means accepting these new roles? Is Sandy interested in working on the marriage now that she can support herself?" The group waited patiently for Jake to speak.

"Like the Marines, Do We Need a Few Good Men?"

Contesting the Single-Sex Mandate of the YWCA

Lynn M. Harter, Erika L. Kirby,
and Margaret M. Quinlan

KEY TERMS

- ◆ social movements
- ◆ feminist organizing
- ◆ (reverse) sexism
- ◆ inclusiveness
- ◆ discrimination

After returning from dropping baby Claire off at daycare, Grace took a few minutes to herself and slowly sipped her morning cup of green tea infused with ginger and peppermint. Her physician had told her both herbs helped to calm nerves, and she certainly needed that now. She absent-mindedly drummed her fingers against the file on her kitchen table labeled *YWCA Board Notes*. In a few hours, she and the other board members of the local Middleton Young Women's Christian Association (YWCA) would decide whether to retain, revise, or reject its single-sex mandate—a mandate in place for affiliates around the globe since the inception of the first YWCA in 1855. The single-sex mandate limits official membership to women and girls and prohibits the inclusion of men on boards of directors. It was critical that the board reach its decision today so its two elected delegates could vote on behalf of the Middleton YWCA affiliate at the upcoming annual convention of the YWCA of the U.S.A. This decision was not an easy one for the local board. In fact, during the past three board meetings, members had failed to reach a consensus and the core issues and values at play remained highly contested. Grace left the previous board meetings distracted, finding it difficult to nurse Claire, and unable to eat or sleep herself.

As she looked out at her flower garden and noted the morning dew that often accompanied the humidity (and mosquitoes) of Minnesota summers, she recounted the numerous positions taken up by various board members. The differing views seemed to revolve around questions like, "How can we best organize ourselves in response to the inequities that continue to be experienced by women and girls? Who should be allowed to participate in social movements inspired by gender and sex discrimination? How viable is a membership policy that prohibits men from participating in organizational governance? Ultimately, who should decide membership rules of local affiliates of an international organization?"

Before she began her morning routine, Grace pondered these questions in light of her experience on the board and paging through her *YWCA Board Notes* file. She knew that for the past 150 years, YWCAs in the United States have raised awareness about gendered inequities and provided material and social support for women and girls. The Middleton affiliate with which Grace was involved has organized a rape and abuse crisis center, a homeless shelter, a daycare center, leadership training programs, and health and fitness programs. Grace knew from her orientation to the Board that the YWCAs of Britain, Norway, Sweden, and the United States founded the World YWCA in 1894, which now includes affiliates in Asia, Africa, and South America. Her file still held the PowerPoint handout that familiarized her with many facts about the World YWCA.

♦ The World YWCA unites 25 million women in over 122 countries through 100 affiliated national YWCAs.

♦ These affiliates are joined by their desire to support the efforts of women across the borders of nations and states as they work toward economic, political, physical, and social liberation.

♦ Nationally and internationally, YWCAs work toward social change through legislative and development initiatives.

♦ YWCAs have raised health awareness about HIV and AIDS and breast cancer, advocated healthy lifestyles through fitness programs, sponsored hostels in conflict and post-conflict regions, and created sanitation systems and agricultural projects in developing countries.

As Grace reviewed the evolution of YWCAs, she reflected, "It's amazing how affiliates have remained organizations led *by* women and *for* women and children. This membership structure has been successful on many fronts in rectifying gendered discrimination and has provided space for women to develop leadership skills and organize for their own empowerment." But several years ago, a group of Executive Directors of the YWCA of the United States raised questions as to why the YWCA as a movement was not progressing. In response, the Transition Team Steering Committee of the national board distributed a strategic plan to the 300 affiliated chapters in the United States; it was one of the documents in Grace's file.[1] The plan included three alternative positions as to whether or not to retain the single-sex membership mandate of the organization:

1. Local affiliates should be allowed to structure both membership and governance in ways that advance their organizational visions.
2. The single-sex membership policy should be retained for all affiliates of the YWCA in the United States.
3. Membership should be opened up to men, but roles in governance should not be opened to men.

Each local board had been asked to debate these positions and send representatives from their local affiliate to the national convention ready to vote for one approach on behalf of their board. Paper clipped to that strategic plan, Grace found a copy of an article from the *Albuquerque Journal,*[2] where Peggy Sanchez Mills, CEO of the YWCA in the United States had declared, "The goal is to keep the whole united. But when you join a national organization, you accept certain standards." It was clear the organization wanted to adopt one position for all the affiliates to follow. Grace wondered, "Which of these three options is best? There are so many things that need to be considered when making this decision—thinking about history, about the political climate, about gendered dynamics—it's a lot to get my head around."

She remembered Emily's poignant contribution at the last board meeting: "The pioneers of this organization came of age at times and in societies that were quite unprepared and even unwilling to allow women space for collective contributions or participation outside of rigidly defined roles in private spheres. Yet, times are different now."

Local sentiment seemed to agree with Emily; a recent article from a local newspaper quipped, "Like the marines, doesn't the YWCA need a few good men?"[3] The journalist and several community members accused the local board of reverse discrimination and suggested the time has come for the YWCA to allow men to become members in order to participate more fully in addressing sex-based discrimination. As Grace reflected on the article, she could not help but think about her daughter and envision the kind of world she hoped Claire would

grow up in. "What impacts might the decision we make today have for generations to come in the United States as well as globally?"

As Grace attempted to clarify her own position amongst the three alternatives, she pulled out the minutes of the last board meeting from the file. Gabrielle,
the President of the local board, had begun the meeting by reading from the strategic plan the technicalities of how "the single-sex mandate of the YWCA has been
upheld by the U.S. Supreme Court as supported by the compensatory purpose
doctrine. This doctrine has been used in other cases as well to uphold single-sex
classifications when the sex-based classification is adopted with the intention of
helping members who have been disadvantaged, such as women. The U.S.
Supreme Court continues to uphold single-sex classifications which counteract
societal disadvantages women have experienced and that are designed to aid
women in achieving equality with men."

To this, Emily had countered, "Even if the mandate is legally defensible,
YWCA affiliates in communities across the United States are starting to experience resistance to these exclusionary membership policies. The Supreme Court
may allow us to continue with this policy, but our own members and other community organizations do not have to support it. And, quite frankly, we depend on
the resources available within our local community." Reading Emily's comments
in the minutes reinforced for Grace that the needs and demands of local con-
stituents of YWCA affiliates must be considered in this decision—not only those
served by the programs and those who financially support the programs.

Emily had certainly offered compelling arguments in favor of opening membership and governance to include men at the last board meeting. She had stressed
that "Our stated values of diversity and inclusiveness will be more widely
respected by the communities we serve if we discontinue the categorical exclusion of men. Our current exclusion of men is seen as a contradiction to our commitment to non-discrimination, and members of our community are starting to
voice this concern." Indeed, a local newspaper article recently opened with the
line, "For the YWCA, whose masthead reads 'empowering women,' a penalty for
discrimination could be a fairly bitter pill to swallow."[4]

Numerous board members had expressed hesitancy about the need for an
exclusionary membership and governance policy—Grace read her own question
in the minutes of the last meeting: "While the single sex mandate was clearly
important in the United States in the late nineteenth and early twentieth century,
is it still integral to advancing our mission today?"

Gabrielle, who was of the opinion that the single-sex mandate should stay,
was quick to respond, "If we open our leadership to men, are we unintentionally

communicating that we need their support? Will such a move potentially misdirect attention away from issues of relevance for women and girls? There continues to be something powerful about women closing the door and sitting around a board room and self-identifying issues of importance to them."

Grace reflected on the meeting minutes in light of other information provided to board members. The *Albuquerque Journal* article reported how in the past five years, two local YWCA chapters disaffiliated from the YWCA in the United States due to its exclusionary membership policy. One changed its policy due to the threat of loss of funds and the other could not join a human rights organization due to the national organization's single-sex membership policy. Ten other chapters had defied the national mandate by changing their local by-laws to include men, and in so doing risked expulsion or other punitive outcomes. "These 12 chapters must have experienced tremendous social, political, and financial pressures within their local communities about their exclusionary policies to take such a big risk in deciding to enlarge their membership and governance policies to men," Grace contemplated.

Such pressures were echoed in the article; discriminatory practices were targeted by multiple city councils across the nation who passed laws preventing organizations (like YWCAs) from using city-wide facilities such as community centers and from receiving funds for projects if their policies and practices adversely impacted categorical groupings of people like men. Grace paused to consider her own board's recent communication with the United Way, a primary funder of many of their projects including the homeless shelter. In other communities, the United Way has taken action to deny funding to all nonprofit organizations that practiced any form of discrimination. "Would we be able to sustain our work if we lost the credibility and support of funders like United Way?" she wondered. As she tried to summarize these conditions, Grace concluded, "The single-sex mandate is being reexamined in light of the circumstances of many local YWCAs in the United States. If the national board does not change its policy, it may leave many local YWCA boards, like Middleton's, to make a choice between solidarity and connection with a global movement and organizational network on one hand and access to local resources on the other."

Grace found that Emily's arguments were really starting to sway her, and so she decided to reread more of Gabrielle's comments to get a counterpoint. When Emily had made the comment that the Supreme Court might allow discrimination but that local communities would not, Gabrielle had reminded all of them that "We must consider the contemporary needs of women both at home and abroad. Some women served by YWCAs in countries other than our own continue to experience very restrictive cultural norms. And like it or not, the votes and opinions of the YWCA in the United States—and the example it sets—remains a pivotal axis on which the World YWCA turns. So what we decide has broader implications than just affecting U.S. American women and girls."

And at another point in the meeting Grace found comments where Gabrielle had cautioned, "I hate to keep coming back to this, but I feel a need to advocate for those who are not here to advocate for themselves. We need to think about the YWCA worldwide and not just in the United States. Perhaps empowerment for women here in Middleton does demand working with men to fight racism or other evils—but in the Middle East and other parts of the globe the inclusion of men could usher in all sorts of additional oppression or disrupt the perceived 'safe haven' or 'sanctuary' that the YWCA represents in being women-only. I believe that if U.S. chapters change to include men, YWCA affiliates worldwide might feel pressure to follow. Do we really want to take that risk?"

Grace thought about some reading she was doing about global feminist communities. She had learned that even though there are no "essential" qualities that women and men across nation states, generations, and races share that bind them to a common cause, this does not preclude the establishment of connections among diverse peoples. Yet changing the single-sex mandate just might erode those connections. As Grace loaded her business tote with the *YWCA Board Notes* file, she typed a note in her smartphone before tossing it in the bag: "YWCA organizations in the United States are struggling to both claim and own their local contexts alongside the demands of affiliation with a global movement, so how can local affiliates make their own calls on who can participate while still working with chapters in other countries in a celebration of diversity, mutual respect, equality, and dignity for the human spirit?" Grace shook her head as she realized she had been going around in circles in her own head for the past two hours, and even though she was still unclear about which option she would support, it was time to get going to the meeting.

endnotes

1. YWCA. (2001). *Ten steps to absolute change transition plan.* Washington, DC: Author.
2. Honaberger, W. J. (2003, December 9). Local YWCA wants to add men. *Albuquerque Tribune.*
3. Cook, D. (2000, January 7). Like Marines, YWCA also needs a few good men. *Business Journal of Portland.*

"Our Father Creator Who Art in Heaven . . ."

Negotiating Patriarchy in Religion and Feminism

Erika L. Kirby

KEY TERMS

- ◆ patriarchy
- ◆ institutional power
- ◆ socialization
- ◆ inclusive language

Throughout her adult life, Heather had periodically struggled to reconcile being both a Catholic and a feminist. Her sister, who had left the church, often smirked, "I just don't get it. You are a feminist, a GLBT[1] (gay-lesbian-bisexual-transgender) ally, and a pro-choice supporter—and a Catholic? One of the most patriarchal institutions in existence, where in some archdiocese women can't even be on the altar, let alone be priests or deacons. Don't you see the contradiction? How do you reconcile that in your mind?" After 12 years of Catholic schooling, they had both learned that Heather's multiple identities did not completely jive, yet somehow, she was usually able to bracket the institution from her day-to-day spiritual life. To be sure, some interactions brought the issue to the forefront more than others, and this week the inconsistencies between her feminist identity and norms of Catholicism again needed to be managed—this time for her daughter's benefit.

As Heather pondered the current situation, her thoughts drifted back 15 years: "The last time I had to decide how much to push for my feminist ideals was in our marriage preparation." She recalled vividly the meeting where they designed the ceremony with the priest. While Heather was planning to change her name to that of her husband-to-be, she had battled with Father Joseph about announcing them as "Tony and Heather McCoy" rather than his preference of "Mr. and Mrs. Anthony McCoy." And there were other aspects of the ceremony that Heather felt should break with more "traditional" wedding rituals; she wanted both her mother and her father to walk her down the aisle and had refused several choices of readings offered by Fr. Joseph. "I will *not* begin our life together using a reading where a woman is a mere afterthought made from a man's rib," she held firm.

In response, Fr. Joseph had said, "Well, I want you to take a good look how you have been pushing your choices today. Think about the future—if there is a divorce in your family, *it will be your fault* because you speak out too much and don't let Tony make all the decisions."

Fast forward 15 years, and Heather had now been through other sacramental preparations as a parent for Baptism and Reconciliation (confession), and they had begun preparations for Mia's first Eucharist (communion) later that year. So they had been working diligently memorizing the "required" prayers. Heather replayed the conversation that had led to her current dilemma in her head. She had been practicing the *Our Father* with Mia when she suddenly asked, "But Mommy, that's not how you say it. Why do you say it different?"

"That's a good question, Mia," Heather remembered taking a breath and then stammering a bit in her reply. She did not realize Mia had picked up on her replacement of "Creator" for "Father" in formal prayers. She also regularly substituted "people" for "man" and at times even called the Holy Spirit a "she." Sometimes she got curious stares at Mass, but it was a commitment she was willing to defend for herself. "Remember when you asked me 'Where are all the girl priests?' a few years ago? Do you remember what we talked about?"

"Sure, you said God loves girls as much as boys, but sometimes the ways that people think we should do things in our church doesn't show it . . . you used some big word . . ."

"You have such a good memory!" Heather congratulated her. "That word was patriarchy . . . Well, since I'm not sure that God *is* a man, I don't use the word 'Father,' and instead I use 'Creator.'" And Mia then made the proclamation that she did not expect.

"Okay. Well I'm not sure either so I'm gonna say it like you and practice my prayer with 'Our Creator' too," Mia announced matter-of-factly.

In the moment, Heather had just smiled, but she knew this was a serious matter. "Should I let Mia practice and recite the prayer 'incorrectly' and allow her to give her feminist explanation to the teacher or priest? What will the consequences of that be? Should I tell Mia that while we believe this at home, she should say it 'right' for her teacher? What kind of message does that send?" Heather hoped for some clarity soon, because the recitation of the *Our Father/Creator* was scheduled for Catechetics in two days.

endnote

1. GLBT (also LGBT): either of these expressions are acronyms for individuals who are gay, lesbian, bisexual, or transgender/transsexual. The acronym differs across organizations; for example, the Human Rights Campaign (HRC) utilizes GLBT while the Gay, Lesbian and Straight Education Network (GLSEN) utilizes LGBT.

"If a Boy Is Playing with It, It's a Boy Toy; If a Girl Is Playing with It, It's a Girl Toy"

Questioning the Gendering of Toys

Paaige K. Turner

KEY TERMS

- toys
- stereotypes
- socialization
- language

"Why would he say that?" Janice thought to herself as she listened to the conversation of the three boys playing with her nine-year-old son in his room.

As a feminist mother, Janice knew she wanted her two children, Elizabeth and Justin, to choose who they wanted to be as men and women. At the same time, she understood her son and daughter would grow up in a world that would saturate them with messages about how boys and girls should behave. Just watching the toy ads on television alone was enough to make her worry. She found herself muttering, "Boys always play aggressively with trucks, action figures, sports equipment, and war toys, and girls always sit nicely as they groom themselves and their dolls or prepare food to serve to the family."

Janice was sure it would not be enough to just tell them not to believe the ads. She had to find a way to replace the images they saw with an alternative interpretation and develop skills to negotiate the situations in which they found themselves. "Sort of like the 'Say no to drugs' campaign" she thought, "Don't do it and here are things you can say when you find yourself in a bad situation." Hmmm . . . what if the toy was defined not by what it was, but by who played with it? Her kids would see that it was the culture that dictated who got to do what and then they would feel free to choose whatever toy, or life, they wanted! Their family mantra became "If a boy is playing with it, it's a boy toy; if a girl is playing with it, it's a girl toy." At every opportunity, Janice pointed out how boys and girls were directed towards gender-appropriate toys.

"Can I take your order?" asked the fast food cashier.

"Yes, we would like two chicken nugget kid's meals," replied Janice.

"Would you like boy toys or girl toys with that?"

"I would like trucks," said Janice.

"Boy toys," said the cashier.

"No, trucks," said Janice

"Yea, boy toys," said the cashier.

"No, I want trucks, not boy toys," insisted Janice.

"I want the boy toy," said Bruce, Justin's best friend.

"It'll be okay, you'll get the right toy," said Justin to his friend. "It's just that she doesn't like that they think only boys play with trucks. See, it isn't really a boy toy, it's a truck that is played with by boys."

"That's right, Bruce," confirmed Janice. "What if a girl wanted the truck or the boy wanted the doll? How would asking for a 'boy toy' make a girl feel? Or asking for a 'girl toy' make a boy feel?"

While Bruce seemed perplexed, Janice felt proud that her son had a clear understanding of the implications of labeling specific toys as inherently boy or girl as well as the tools to explain himself.

Janice jumped from her thoughts back into the present where the boys were playing in the bedroom. "Hey, why do you have a Hello Kitty doll on your bed?" Justin had three friends over that day, Dustin, Izaha, and Stanley. They were not really close friends but the four of them played together on the soccer team and invited each other to their birthday parties. When Janice heard the question, she slowed her pace and stepped to the side of the door, out of view. Justin had specifically saved that Hello Kitty doll last month from his sister Elizabeth's Goodwill box exclaiming, "She's too cute to give away." Janice listened intently.

"Oh, she's soft and good for hitting. See?" said Justin. Janice could hear Justin hitting the doll. "Want to go outside?" asked Justin. Janice watched them file out of the room in stunned silence wondering what had just happened and what to do next. Should she follow them and explain about boy toys and girl toys? Wait to talk to her son later? Ignore it? Janice would have to figure out what she wanted to do.

33

"Let Me Work the Kinks Out of Your Neck"

The Story of Jared and Chris

Diana K. Ivy and Shawn T. Wahl

KEY TERMS

♦ sexual harassment
♦ discrimination (workplace)
♦ hostile environment
♦ nonverbal communication
♦ cross-sex interactions

"Here we go—a new day, a new city, a new apartment, and a new job," Jared thought to himself. He felt like a new person, starting fresh, just out of college, with everything to look forward to and no regrets, other than how much he indulged himself at his after-graduation party. Even that seemed like a fond, distant memory now, since he had moved to the "big city" (a far cry from the small college town where he had been living the last four years). Jared looked forward to meeting a lot of new people and launching what he just knew would be a lucrative career in sales.

Jared was fairly successful in college—not a "Dean's Lister" by any means, but not a slacker either. He graduated with an acceptable GPA, enjoyed (most of) his major and his professors, and felt like his courses, along with the internships and part-time jobs, prepared him well for a future in business. He was smart about finding a job too, using the career center on campus, getting good references from employers and his favorite profs, sending out resumés way before his friends even thought to work on theirs, and using contacts he had made along the way to network himself into a career. Landing a great job was hard work, but Jared's efforts paid off when he was hired at his dream job.

In terms of social life, Jared dated a few women casually while in college, but not seriously, preferring to hang out with friends than become committed to anyone. He knew himself too well: his career came first. He enjoyed the company of women, but he was a man on a professional mission—not a social one.

After graduating, moving, and getting settled in his new place, Jared knew it was time to get down to business—literally. His first two weeks on the new job were not going to be anything like what he would eventually be doing because he had to go through the company's orientation and training program conducted by the Human Resources (HR) Department. But he thought with anticipation, "After the program, I'll be assigned to a division with a supervisor and coworkers, and then I'll be off and running. For now, I just need to concern myself with all these policies and forms on boring subjects like health insurance and the company retirement plan. What do I care about retirement? I'm just getting started. . . ."

Jared had taken a human resources management course in college—what was generally referred to as the "personnel" course—so he understood the significance of policies that affect the day-to-day operations of any firm, as well as the long-range health of an organization. The HR course covered such prickly topics as workplace ethics, employee privacy and security, sexual harassment, and discrimination in the workplace related to sex, race/ethnicity, age, religion, and so forth. The legal implications of these issues were mind-boggling, especially to Jared's classmates, who had little work experience before graduation. But Jared felt like he had a pretty good grasp of the issues and understood how to avoid the pitfalls that sometimes afflict new, young, unattached employees.

Jared put his head down, studied the HR material, and finished the training session with flying colors. Finally, he was assigned to a unit with a supervisor named Chris and an office on the 17th floor. He started his work day exceptionally early that first Monday morning after training so that he could make a good impression on his coworkers and, especially, his boss. He hoped this guy, Chris, was someone he could relate to and get along with well; the last thing he needed was a jerk for a boss. Jared fired up his computer and checked his schedule, noting that he had an 11:00 A.M. meeting with his "team"—the company's vernacular for the boss and the workers in a particular unit. He then started reviewing the company's online quarterly sales reports.

After a few hours of staring intently into a computer screen, Jared felt his neck and shoulders stiffen—he had been sitting at his desk, basically in one position, for over two hours. As he moved his neck back and forth and shrugged his shoulders to get the circulation going again, he heard footsteps behind his chair.

Someone had slipped into his office while he was focused on his computer and was now massaging his shoulders. When Jared moved away—part shocked, part embarrassed—he turned around and looked up to find a very attractive woman, probably mid thirties, dressed professionally, looking down at him and smiling.

"You're new here, aren't you? Jared, right? Well turn back around, Jared, and let me work the kinks out of your neck here, so you can go into your meeting in a few minutes less stressed out." She turned his chair back around to face the computer and began working on his neck and shoulders once more. Jared had to hand it to her—she was convincing and persistent—so he let her return to her massage, feeling better as the soreness went away. While touching him, she talked about what was on his computer screen. She moved on to discussing sales projections and trends and then new products on the horizon that looked promising for the company.

Jared thought, "If she knows I have a meeting in a few minutes, I must be working with her in some capacity. I hope she's a coworker because she really knows her stuff! She seems to have a good business sense about her. And she's *so* attractive—almost like out of a magazine!" He also secretly hoped that she was not his administrative assistant.

After about 10 minutes of this activity (the woman massaging, Jared letting her massage him, all the while talking business), she said, "Well, I need to get going now; see you soon." She strode out of his office just as quickly as she made her way in. He sat there, reviewing what had happened and realizing that he never got her name. She did all the talking; he did not even have a chance for a formal introduction.

"Well, this is a friendly company. I'm really going to like it here," were Jared's thoughts as he gathered his laptop and coat and headed down to the conference room at the end of the hall for his first meeting with his team.

Jared's "teammates" gathered in the conference room; lots of handshakes and introductions were exchanged, with people working hard to make a good impression, while trying to remember the name of the person they just met. Then the room got quiet. Imagine Jared's shock when the attractive "masseuse" who had been in his office earlier entered the conference room, introduced herself as Chris, the team manager, and started introductions around the table. Jared stumbled out his name when his turn came, still in a state of disbelief, feeling like a trick had been played on him by his new boss. Chris showed no "knowing" expression on her face when Jared introduced himself, no hint that anything had transpired between them, no indication that she had knowledge of him that was any different than that of other colleagues in the room. Jared talked to himself, "Calm down—you're overreacting to a mild flirtation that probably wasn't a flirtation at all. What you really need to do is stop thinking so much and start listening" because the boss was talking a mile a minute. At the very least, Jared found their interaction to be a bewildering start to a professional relationship.

As the weeks progressed and Jared came to know his job and teammates better, he enjoyed the work, still convinced that he made the right decision to join the company. But there was a definite down side. There had been more "incidents" with Chris. She never did anything overtly in the company of other people, like teammates or assistants. Jared had tried to avoid being alone with Chris, but in those rare occasions where they were alone, she asked Jared questions about his personal and sexual life—was he dating anyone, sleeping with anyone, did he even like girls—inappropriate questions right out of the samples in the training manual! Chris' actions were uncomfortable for Jared as well, in that she often got too close to him when they talked in his office or hers, she tended to brush up against him when she knew no one was looking, like in crowded elevators, and the shoulder massages continued on occasion. The unwanted attention was starting to affect his ability to concentrate on his work; his self-esteem was plummeting, and his excitement for work was flattening. No one at work ever said anything to Jared about the situation, mainly because they did not know and Jared did not think he had close enough relationships with any of them to say anything. In Jared's mind, Chris was "careful and slick," meaning that her flirtatious actions toward him were always accomplished in private—no witnesses. In fact, he was not sure if Chris even realized the error of her ways.

One night when Jared decided to work late, Chris came into his office, circled around his desk, and started the same old shoulder massage behavior. This time Jared stood up, looked her in the eye, and said, "please stop, Chris" as gently and professionally as he could. He added, "it makes me feel a little strange when you do that, like you're giving me special attention or something."

Chris looked puzzled and a little bit angry at first, and then she gave Jared a wry, knowing smile and left his office without saying anything. She behaved for a few weeks as if he had the plague and then things leveled off. But then the attention started up again, as if Chris either did not believe Jared's protests or did not recognize that her own behavior was harassment. From Jared's perspective, she just "didn't get it."

When Jared would let himself think about it, he got angry: "What made Chris think it was okay to treat me this way? She's older than I am and is supposed to be some sort of mentor, but she crosses the line every chance she gets. Was she personal like this with all the male employees? Perhaps even the female employees?"

He didn't delude himself that he was special or singled out for Chris' attention because he knew people who behaved this way tended to be "equal opportunity offenders," meaning they were inappropriate with just about anyone. The odd thing was that Chris was well-respected by her superiors at the company; her track record was impeccable in terms of sales productivity. The men in upper management seemed to be grooming Chris for a promotion, which made the situation all the more bewildering. As far as Jared knew, Chris had never been reported for bad behavior by anyone at the company, but he doubted that he was the first subordinate with whom she had been inappropriate.

Then Jared remembered something that happened back in college. A friend, Sabrina, was having trouble with a graduate teaching assistant (TA); the male TA was showing her too much attention during lab sessions and making her feel weird. She thought it was sexual harassment, but was reluctant to report the TA. She did not want to make a big deal of it but just wanted to tell someone what was happening. He remembered Sabrina telling him, "my sorority had a campus speaker on sexual harassment, who stressed that the most important first step for people who think they've been harassed is to tell someone they trust what happened, just to get the situation out of their own head and make it real." Now Jared reflected on this lesson about the importance of telling someone his story, even if he might not want any action taken. He could not believe that he was now placed in Sabrina's situation, only with a twist: Jared was the male target of a female harasser.

Should that make a difference? Jared wondered, "Do sexual harassment policies work the same when *men* are the targets of *women*'s attention? If the laws were applied equitably, what kind of heat would he take if he reported Chris' inappropriate behavior?" He still had trouble labeling it sexual harassment because there was no "quid pro quo"—no direct threats if he refused Chris' overtures. It was more subtle than that. In fact, when Jared confronted Chris about it, she had not even said anything before walking out of the room. Was he overthinking the situation and overreacting to Chris' come-ons? After all, Sabrina's situation seemed more typical but now here he was—a *guy,* getting harassed by a *woman.* He knew that if he told any of his male colleagues what was happening that he would likely get a macho reaction—they would tease him, call him "teacher's pet," and some would even suggest that he "go for it," since, after all, Chris was very attractive. Just last week at a happy hour after work, he heard one of his coworkers, Terrell, say, "Man, did you see how hot Chris was today?" Jonah replied, "Yeah, and she's single. I wonder what kind of men she goes for." All of that talk made Jared uncomfortable, and he never joined in with the banter.

Jared got so off his game because of the situation with his boss that he began doubting his own instincts and perceptions of events, which caused him to be less effective on the job. He kept thinking about Chris' treatment of him: "Was it a textbook case of sexual harassment, or was it something else? Was it really that big of a deal, just a little massage, a little extra attention, colleague to colleague? Did I contribute in any way to making Chris believe her actions were welcome? If someone scrutinized my behavior in the months I've been on the job, would I be blameless? Did I send mixed signals by not telling Chris to back off that very first time she massaged me and contribute to my own harassment?"

Next came a million questions as to what to do, if anything: Should he blow the whistle on his boss, labeling her behavior sexual harassment and filing an internal grievance with the company's HR Department? Since Chris had more standing and track record with the company than Jared, should he go around the internal grievance process, head straight for the Equal Employment Opportunity Commission, and file an official complaint? Maybe he should back up a bit and just try to have another talk with Chris, one-on-one, to set her straight on what he would and would not put up with as her employee. If they did talk, should he threaten a grievance or even a lawsuit, just to give Chris the strongest message possible? Is threatening your boss like that ever a good idea? Should he tell a friend—someone not associated with the company—about what was going on, just to get another viewpoint? What were his rights as a new employee? He needed to figure out best course of action, given that—despite how his boss treated him— he really did like his job and the company. Plus he had just moved away from family and friends to this new city and a lot was riding on his success on the job. How could he face his parents and tell them what happened at his "dream job," after they'd been so proud he landed it? Should Jared risk his career, just because his boss, Chris, could not keep her hands to herself?

Making Ourselves a(t) Home in Academia

The "Creatively Welcoming" Space of OSCLG

*Cynthia Berryman-Fink, Cheris Kramarae,
Bobby Patton, Anita Taylor, and
Virginia E. Wheeless[1]*

KEY TERMS

- ◆ feminist organizing
- ◆ empowerment
- ◆ inclusiveness
- ◆ social movements
- ◆ patriarchy
- ◆ discrimination

1973: AnaMaria dropped her suitcase on the bed and grabbed an apple from the fridge. After flying all day from one coast of the United States to the other, she was starving. She had just returned from the annual convention of the Speech Communication Association (SCA),[1] disillusioned by everything associated with "the academy"—especially the closed-minded reactions to her quest to pursue issues of sex in communication for her dissertation research.[2] Feeling quite alone, she sought comfort in her books. She found her copy of Betty Freidan's *The Feminine Mystique* on the shelf and plopped on the couch. She doubted she would reread any of it, but just holding it made her feel better.

AnaMaria closed her eyes and replayed a scene from the meeting in her head. When feeling unsupported like this, her comfort had always been telling herself, "Right now you are still a student. Someday you will have your doctorate, and then things will be easier. People will actually listen to you when you push for inclusive language. They won't just roll their eyes."

So she had been shocked to witness that panel on *Attitude Change* at the SCA convention. As was typical, a panel of male scholars talked about their research in this "traditional" area (in fact, AnaMaria was being pushed to do her dissertation research on some aspect of persuasion and not include anything about sex differences). A discussion ensued at the end when the session was opened for the question/answer period. At one point in the discussion, a woman AnaMaria knew—a female scholar with a doctorate whom she admired very much—raised her hand and commented from the back of the room: "I am a little concerned that you are all talking only about 'he,' 'his,' 'him,' and 'men,' as if only men do communicative actions. Couldn't we use more inclusive language such as 'she and he,' and 'women and men' to help remind everyone that women are also communicators?" AnaMaria remembered nodding her head in agreement—and looking around to notice no one else was doing so. There was a brief silence, then discussion resumed as if the woman had never "interrupted."

AnaMaria thought to herself, "I can't imagine . . .'unwelcomed' would seem to be an understatement of how isolated that woman must have felt! Why does no one else seem to have an interest in this critical issue of sex and language?" As a feminist graduate student who was trying to build a research program for her own work in that area, AnaMaria was getting used to receiving limited support for her ideas—and indeed her identity. In her day-to-day life as a graduate student, she was often treated as a woman first, student second. Even before she was admitted to graduate school, AnaMaria recalled how a professor in the admission interview had asked, "Are you married or engaged?" and "Do you plan have children?" He followed with a rationale: "Our program doesn't want to waste a graduate fellowship on a less than serious scholar."

AnaMaria recollected that when she arrived on campus, she had been discouraged from her plan to study communication and sex. She found no faculty mentors as well as no attention to women in course content. In her four years of graduate school in communication, AnaMaria had encountered just two female professors. Her university had neither a women's center nor a safe space for sexual minorities. And while there was a new Black Studies program on campus, there was no Women's Studies program, although one had been established recently at San Diego State University.[3] And because she really wanted to teach courses involving attention to sex in communication, she had been doing some investigation and had learned that fewer than 41 gender communication courses (or parts of courses) were then offered, and these at only 29 U.S. colleges or universities.

In the absence of attention to women in the communication curricula, few people recognized the need for research questions in this area. Most scholarship in communication showcased men or included only men among the respondents. Few studies included any discussion about gender in communication. In the few studies that did include some women, the researchers did not look explicitly at how different perceptions of sex impacts communication or provide any theoretical grounding for considering sex differences. They did not discuss sex differences as a part of the research but only as an after-thought as the data were mined for some "significant" findings.

AnaMaria knew that outside university settings, women were asking serious questions about the treatment of women in many areas. She had asked her committee to approve dissertation research on perceptions of women's language use, but her all-male dissertation committee dismissed the idea. One professor warned, "What you want to do may be interesting, but it isn't communication." Another professor added, "I'd like to be able to write a good letter of recommendation for you when you apply for a job," implying that he would not be able, or willing, to do that if she did not fit her research plans into more conventional disciplinary categories. Even a seemingly sympathetic faculty member advised her to deal with "real" communication issues at least until she had a degree, a good job, and tenure.

AnaMaria kept thinking about that scene at the convention. In some ways it reflected the turbulence, unrest, and disjointedness she was often hearing and seeing around her in these early 1970s. She knew that many women of all ages were talking about women's liberation. Even her own mother had said, "The personal is political," pointing out how women's personal lives are political because they reflect a sexist power structure. Women held few leadership positions and had relatively little economic power in society. Women and men worked in largely different occupations and women earned significantly less than men. Few high schools or colleges offered more than token sports opportunities. Most people still considered rape an act of lust not an act of violence and control. Domestic violence was regarded as a private matter. Newspaper classified advertisements specified women's jobs and men's jobs.

Yes, there were people both outside and within the academic settings speaking up for equality and inclusivity of all sexual orientations. Many women were advocating for reproductive freedom and calling attention to the full range of women's health issues. Many women were discussing their frustrations at often being subjected to annoying, sometimes hostile intimidation, coercion, and exploitation based on their sex (the term "sexual harassment" had not yet been coined). Some critics were documenting the uses and effects of sexist language.

But far too often such advocates for women's equality were labeled as extremists or radicals. "Women's libbers" had become an epithet. Too many people saw no problem with continued preferential treatment of men.

In short, while there was a push for equality, it had certainly not been achieved. This made for lonely times for the students and faculty who saw critical communication questions and problems but could find few or no allowable way to research or address them in their academic settings. At the convention, AnaMaria had heard of some faculty members who were denied credit and tenure for their work on women's issues, and she knew of graduate students who had been ridiculed and denied credit for their work on sex differences in communication. Convention presentations included few papers discussing language and sex differences research, and the panel she attended was not the only place such ideas were dismissed. But AnaMaria had *some* hope. She knew a group in SCA had just formed a Women's Caucus, and she had learned that several graduate students at Stanford University were starting a newsletter to help those interested to learn about others' research dealing with gender and communication and about meetings where such topics could be discussed. AnaMaria eagerly anticipated the first issue.

1978: AnaMaria rushed with her bags to catch a taxi to the hotel. Tomorrow was a landmark event—a meeting called the *Conference on Communication, Language and Sex* at Bowling Green State University in Bowling Green, Ohio that Cindy Berryman, a graduate student, and Virginia Eman (Wheeless), a faculty member, had planned. They had issued a call for a meeting "to bring together scholars of gender and language who were isolated at their respective universities in environments that questioned the legitimacy of research and teaching about gender in order to facilitate professional and personal networking and provide informal opportunities for dialogue about research and teaching about gender."

Checking into the hotel, AnaMaria met some of the other conference attendees, who invited her to eat with them. Finally, she thought, a chance to talk freely with others about language/sex issues, and she was not disappointed. At dinner and the meetings that followed, the attendees engaged in lively conversations and explored ways to advance scholarship about what by this time they were calling "gender issues in communication." They talked about possible courses, curricula changes, and resource materials to use—films as well as books. When this stimulating interdisciplinary conference came to an end, AnaMaria was sad. But participants had promised to keep in touch, and in a brainstorming session had offered many ideas for how to continue these gatherings. A name was even suggested: The *Organization for the Study of Communication, Language and Gender* (OSCLG).

1979–present: Since that first meeting, AnaMaria has tried to attend an OSCLG conference every year. There have been a few interruptions—birthing her babies and preparing a tenure dossier kept her away. But across the years, she has reported on her research, heard about others' work, shared syllabi and teaching strategies, and discussed how to include the study of gender issues in many communication courses. An important part of all OSCLG meetings has been emphasis on interdisciplinary work, bringing together scholars and teachers from several disciplines (linguistics, communication, sociology, art, psychology, and others). Scholars have met with activists, consultants, and practitioners to discuss theory, ways of teaching, and community activities.

What AnaMaria has loved about the annual conference is that it is usually small—some even call it "boutique-style." Conference planners try to avoid scheduling many concurrent sessions (never more than three at once), so participants have time to talk to each other. They also ensure plenty of hospitality. AnaMaria remembers her friend Cindy—one of those first planners—from the beginning reinforced the importance of food and drink. "There is something to be said for the ideas that can emerge when sipping a great glass of wine," she always declared. And it became a tradition for the president of the organization to hold open houses complete with chocolate and libations after formal meetings end. Overall, attendees appreciate OSCLG's "creatively welcoming" atmosphere. Over the years, conferences have included sessions on mentoring, career challenges, and work-life balance, yoga sessions, guided meditation, karaoke evenings, and other social events that provide time for networking and friendships to develop.

This starkly contrasts with other conferences that have been (not secretly) referred to as "meat markets." The traditional model for academic conferences is a competitive selection of completed papers that authors present, followed by an expert critiquing the research and asking often hostile questions for the author to answer. But OSCLG has embraced a supportive forum for professional discussion, presentation, and publication of research—a collaborative format where tentative ideas could be presented and interested colleagues could follow with intellectual discussion. But beyond this re-imagining of a "traditional" conference in terms of presentations, OSCLG also allows space for performances of poetry and other creative projects. In addition to the peer-reviewed journal *Women and Language,* OSCLG has also published several edited volumes of conference proceedings.

2007: AnaMaria has had a great time at the OSCLG meeting in Omaha, Nebraska. At the board meeting, in her role as OSCLG historian she distributed a list of schools that offer gender studies as part of their communication curriculum.

In compiling that list, she had found courses involving gender in communication in the curriculum of many (if not most) colleges and universities. She smiled in noting that only 29 schools had such offerings when she first made such a list.

On the last day, AnaMaria joined a closing session entitled *Dialogue Embodied* that was created by the conference planners to provide a sense of closure. The session began by identifying what worked during the conference, and quickly turned to conversation about a need to revisit the sense of OSCLG's purpose. As one of the founding members, Cheris Kramarae noted that "The inequalities that were present in the 1970s when OSCLG was created have not disappeared. However, some conditions, including our awareness of what's needed for an equitable society, have changed. We face some important challenges."

AnaMaria asked, "What are those challenges?"

"Well, there are several, most relate to our mission and membership. And organization; could we organize in better ways?" Cheris replied.

Cindy chimed in from across the room, "Yes. For me, one challenge always has been how structured or flexible we should be. When Virginia and I planned that first meeting, we didn't imagine OSCLG would in some ways come to resemble traditional professional organizations with formal bylaws and written rules. I know we work at avoiding becoming a bureaucratic organization that does not foster respect for nonconventional viewpoints; but sometimes I think we're approaching that line."

Virginia added, "And the conference program has gotten so much more formal! I know this is probably necessary so participants can explain the format to university administrators, receive travel funding to attend the conferences, and get résumé credit for their presentations. But such structures can hinder alterative forms of organizing, creativity, and equality of voice and decision making; it's not easy to know how to balance mission and structure."

"For me, another challenge is achieving diverse membership" added Anita. "We have done okay in having diversity in programming. We reach across disciplines fairly well and mix academic and community activities, and we also have performance arts programs and pay attention to innovative research and teaching. But our membership is not very diverse, and as a result our discussions often lack diversity—especially in terms of race, ethnicity, gender, and class. Over the years, white, middle-class women have comprised the majority of members and conference participants."

Bobby agreed: "While I know it is unintentional, ignoring or downplaying the importance of the differences and hierarchies between women, and between men, is a fundamental problem in academe in general, and a lack of sufficient diversity in OSCLG perpetuates this problem even in what is intended to be a more open, egalitarian organization. We need to think about how to foster work that not only thinks about differences, but about intersections of race, gender, class, sexual orientation, and sexual identity." He reminded participants that gender never comes without race, age, class, sexuality, national identity, education, geography, health status, and cultural practices, yet our research and teaching often do not adequately embrace such intersectionality.

"Bobby, you say that so well! All of you are answering AnaMaria's question," Cheris said. "But I see one more thing as a challenge: How do we help new members? How can we do a better job of helping members to move their work from in-progress to publication? How can we mentor individuals as teachers, activists, or practitioners?"

Anita furthered, "And Cheris, your comment about publishing raises another timely issue. As we change editors of *Women and Language,* we need to have an ongoing conversation about how to maintain balance among OSCLG mission and the goals of maintaining quality publication at reasonable costs. We don't want to exclude potential users of our publications. And we're going to need to adapt to a future of publishing that is very much in flux."

AnaMaria added another challenge: "One thing has struck me over the years: I still see women minimized in the public sphere—in the media, in politics, and in even in academia. I think OSCLG needs new ways to monitor and critique society and how it deals with women as they communicate in all aspects of their lives."

The conference planners recorded all these ideas. Some additional questions came up. These included, "What issues confront students and scholars today that could not even be imagined in 1970? How can existing and emerging technologies help OSCLG meet its goals? What could be the role of a website, of blogs, online publishing, and other technologies? How do we foster work that explores the intersections among gender, race, class, sexuality, ethnicities, etc.? How can membership be diversified? What can we do to foster mentoring, networking, and friendship? As it grows in size, how can OSCLG continue to provide personal and professional networking, hospitality, and be welcoming to all participants?" As AnaMaria left, she asked the conference planners to send her their notes. She wanted to start preparing some recommendations to insure that OSCLG continued to be as helpful to future gender scholars as it was to her in 1978. She had a lot of thinking to do before the next conference.

endnotes

1. The authors of this case were instrumental in the founding of the Organization for the Study of Communication, Language, and Gender (OSCLG).

2. The name of the Speech Communication Association was changed to the National Communication Association in 1997; it is an organization headquartered in the United States.

3. When gender in language and communication began to surface as issues of controversy, the word 'gender' was rarely the term of choice. We commented on sexism in language (as in McGraw-Hill's "Guidelines for Equal Treatment of the Sexes" and Casey Miller & Kate Swift's *Words and Women*) or matters related to the sexes in communication (as in Bobby R. Patton *Living together: Female/male communication;* Gene Eakins, Barbara Eakins, and Barbara Lieb-Brilhart [1976]. SISCOM '75: Report of SCA Summer Conference on Men's and Women's Communication; and Barbara Westbrook Eakins and R. Gene Eakins, *Sex Differences in Human Communication*). The inadequacy of such terminology soon became apparent, making gender the term of choice.

4. The first Women's Studies program in the United States had been established at San Diego State University in 1970, although it took several more years to create curriculum, establish governance procedures, and hire faculty.

index of terms

In using this index, the number listed next to a term can be utilized to explore a topic—case numbers are in "regular" format while mini-case numbers are underlined.

A
Ability (<u>14</u>)
Abuse
    Cycle of (15, 29)
    Emotional (2, 15, 29)
    Physical (15, 29)
Adoption (12, 18)
Advertising (*see* Media and Mediated Representations)
Age/Ageism (5, 9, <u>10</u>, <u>25</u>)
Anthropological Theory (*see* Two-Culture Approach)
Appearance (*see* Physical Appearance)
Athletics (*see* Sports)

B
Battering (*see* Abuse)
Beauty, Norms of (*see* Physical Appearance)
Bias (<u>3</u>, 4, 5, <u>13</u>, 23, 24, 33, and also *see* Discrimination)
    In Education (<u>10</u>, 34)
    In Language (1, 5, 22, <u>28</u>, <u>31</u>)
    In Media (<u>7</u>, 33)
    In Policy (4, <u>11</u>, 12, <u>17</u>, 18, 30)
    In Workplace (2, 9, <u>27</u>)
Bible (*see* Religion)
Biological Approaches (2, 9, <u>17</u>, 18, 23, <u>25</u>)
Biology (4, 9, 23, <u>25</u>)
Body Image (6, <u>7</u>, <u>14</u>)
Breadwinner Role (*see* Gendered Roles Home)
Breastfeeding (23)

C

Caregiving (1, <u>13</u>, 18, 19, <u>21</u>, 22, 24)
    Elder (19)
Children (*see* Daughters and Sons)
Class/Classism (*see* Socio-Economic Class)
Classroom Communication (<u>7</u>, <u>10</u>)
Clothing/Dress (5, <u>7</u>, <u>11</u>, <u>14</u>, 22)
Cognitive Development Theory (*see* Identity Formation and Socialization)
Combat, Women in (*see* Military)
Commuter Couple (24)
Cosmetics (<u>11</u>)
Courtship (*see* Dating)
Critical Cultural Approaches to Gender (*see* "Doing" Gender and Standpoint Theory)
Cross-Sex Interactions (2, 9, 26, <u>28</u>, 33)

D

Dating (1, 6, 20)
Daughters (4, 5, <u>8</u>, 12, <u>13</u>, 18, 19, <u>32</u>)
Descriptive Cultural Approaches to Gender (*see* Two-Cultures Approach))
Discrimination (1, 2, 3, <u>11</u>, <u>17</u>, 18, <u>27</u>, 30, 33, 34)
    Workplace (1, 2, <u>27</u>, 33, 34)
Division of Household Labor (<u>13</u>, 19, <u>21</u>, 23, 24, 29)
"Doing" Gender
    Personal Life (6, <u>14</u>, 15, 19, 20, <u>21</u>, 22, 23, 24, <u>28</u>, 29)
    Work Life (2, 9, <u>10</u>, <u>11</u>, <u>17</u>, 22, <u>27</u>, 33, 34)
Domestic Violence (*see* Abuse)
Dominance (1, 2, 15, <u>16</u>, <u>27</u>, <u>28</u>, 29, 30, <u>31</u>, 33, 34)
Double Bind (1, 2, 5, 6, <u>8</u>, <u>17</u>, 18, 19, 20, <u>21</u>, 22, 23, 26, <u>27</u>, <u>28</u>, 30, <u>31</u>)
Dress (*see* Clothing/Dress)
Dual-Career Families (*see* Family)

E

Eating Disorders (6, <u>7</u>)
Education
    As Context (<u>7</u>, <u>11</u>, <u>16</u>, <u>17</u>, <u>28</u>)
    As Topic (<u>10</u>, 22, 34)
    Educating (<u>3</u>, <u>8</u>, 12, <u>28</u>, <u>31</u>, 34)

Empowerment (*see* Power)
Ethnicity (*see* Race)
Exclusionary Language (*see* Language)

F

Family (1, <u>3</u>, 4, 12, <u>13</u>, 18, 19, <u>21</u>, 22, 23, 24) (*see* also Fathering and Mothering)
    Dual-Career Family (1, <u>13</u>, 18, 19, <u>21</u>, 22, 24, <u>25</u>, 26, 29)
    Partner Communication (4, 9, 12, <u>13</u>, 18, 19, 23, 24, 26, 29)
    Parent-Child Communication (4, <u>8</u>, 12, 18, <u>28</u>, <u>31</u>, <u>32</u>)
    Stay-at-Home Parents (*see* Fathering and Mothering)
Fathering (<u>13</u>, 18, 19, <u>21</u>)
    Stay-at-Home (<u>13</u>, 19)
Female-Female Friendship (*see* Friendship)
Femininity/Feminine Style (7, <u>11</u>, <u>14</u>, 20, 22)
Feminism/Feminist Theory (<u>16</u>, <u>31</u>, <u>32</u>, 34)
Feminist Organizing (30, 34)
Friendship
    Cross-Sex (26)
    Same Sex (6, <u>7</u>, 12, 20, 22, 34)

G

Gays (<u>3</u>, 4, 18, <u>28</u>)
Gendered Roles
    Home (<u>8</u>, <u>13</u>, 18, 19, <u>21</u>, 22, 24, <u>25</u>, 29)
    Work (<u>27</u>)
Gendered Labor/Work (1, <u>13</u>, 19, <u>21</u>, 24, 29)
Gendered Violence (*see* Abuse)
Gender Ideals (6, <u>7</u>, <u>11</u>, <u>14</u>, 15, 20, 22, 23, 24, <u>25</u>)
Gender Identity Development (*see* Identity Formation and Socialization)
Gender Reassignment (<u>17</u>)
Gender Socialization (*see* Socialization)
Gender Stereotypes (*see* Stereotypes)
Gender Transition (<u>17</u>)
Generational Issues (5, 9, 23)
Generic (Male) Language (*see* Language)

H

Harassment (*see* Hostile Environment and Sexual Harassment)
Health (4, 6, <u>7</u>, 9, <u>14</u>, 23, <u>25</u>)
    Sexual (4, 9, <u>25</u>)

Heteronormativity (<u>3</u>, 4, 18, 20, 26, <u>28</u>)
Heterosexual Relationships (*see* Marriage and Romantic Relationships)
Homophobia (<u>3</u>, 6, 18, <u>28</u>)
Homosexuals (*see* Gays and Lesbians)
Hostile Environment (2, 23, 26, <u>28</u>, 33)

I

Identity Formation (6, <u>7</u>, 12, <u>13</u>, <u>14</u>, 15, <u>16</u>, <u>17</u>, 18, 20, 30, 34)
Inclusiveness (<u>3</u>, 4, <u>13</u>, <u>17</u>, 30, <u>31</u>, 34)
Inequality and Gender in Institutions (*see* Power, Institutional)
International (12, 30)
Intimate Partner Violence (*see* Abuse)

L

Labor, Division of (*see* Division of Labor)
Language (5, 6, <u>10</u>, <u>16</u>, 26, <u>28</u>, 30, <u>31</u>, <u>32</u>, 34)
Leave Policies (*see* Work-Life Policy)
Lesbians (<u>3</u>, <u>28</u>)
Long-Distance Relationships (*see* Commuter Couple)

M

Male-Male Friendship (*see* Friendship)
Marriage (12, <u>13</u>, 19, 20, <u>21</u>, 24, 26, 29, <u>31</u>)
Masculinity (6, 9, <u>13</u>, 15, 19, <u>28</u>, 29, 33)
Media (4, 5, 19, 22, 23, <u>25</u>, 26, 30)
Mediated Representations (2, 5, 6, <u>7</u>, 20, 23)
Medicine (*see* Health)
Men (*see* Fathering and Masculinity)
Military (2)
Mothering (1, <u>8</u>, 12, 18, <u>21</u>, 22, 23, <u>25</u>, <u>31</u>, <u>32</u>)
    "Mommy Guilt" (1, 12, 22, 23)
    Mommy Track (22)
    Stay-at-Home (<u>21</u>, 22)
Muted Group Theory (34 and *see* Language)

N

Nonverbal Communication (<u>11</u>, 22, 23, 29, 33)

O

Objectification (2, 5, 6, <u>7</u>, <u>11</u>, 33)
Opting Out (22)

P

Parent-Child Communication (*see* Family)
Partner Violence (*see* Abuse)
Patriarchy (2, 5, <u>10</u>, 12, <u>16</u>, 24, <u>27</u>, 30, <u>31</u>, 34)
Patronymy (12)
Performing Gender (*see* "Doing" Gender)
Personal Relationships (*see* Family, Friendships, Marriage, and Romantic Relationships)
Physical Ability (*see* Ability)
Physical Abuse (*see* Abuse)
Physical Appearance (5, 6, <u>7</u>, <u>10</u>, <u>11</u>, <u>14</u>, 15, <u>17</u>, 33)
Platonic Friendships (*see* Friendships, Cross-Sex)
Politics (1, 2, <u>3</u>, 4, 5)
Power (1, 2, <u>3</u>, <u>7</u>, <u>10</u>, 29, 33)
   Empowerment (<u>8</u>, 29, <u>32</u>, 34)
   Institutional (1, 2, 4, <u>11</u>, 12, <u>17</u>, 18, <u>27</u>, 30, <u>31</u>)
   Relational (9, 15, 26, 29, 33)
Privilege (1, <u>14</u>, <u>16</u>, 19, 20, 22)
Psychological Approaches to Gender (*see* Identity Formation and Socialization)

R

Race/Ethnicity as Gender/ed Issue (1, 12, 18, 22)
Racism (1, 5, <u>27</u>)
Relationships (*see* Family, Friendships, Marriage, and Romantic Relationships)
Religion (<u>31</u>)
Reproductive Health (*see* Health, Sexual)
Romance Culture (20, 26)
Romantic Relationship (15, 18, 24, 29)

S

Same-Sex Couples (*see* Gays and Lesbians)
Same-Sex Friendship (*see* Friendship, Same Sex)
Schools (*see* Education)

Self-Esteem (6, <u>7</u>, <u>8</u>, 12, 15, 33)
Sex (4, 6, 9)
Sexism (2, 5, <u>10</u>, <u>11</u>, 12, <u>13</u>, 23, 24, <u>25</u>, <u>27</u>, 30, <u>31</u>, 33, 34)
Sexual Harassment (33)
Sexual Health (*see* Health)
Sexual Orientation (<u>3</u>, 6, 18, <u>28</u>)
Socialization (<u>8</u>, 12, 18, 20, <u>31</u>, <u>32</u>)
Social Learning Theory (*see* Identity Formation and Socialization)
Social Movements (5, 30, 34)
Social Networks (18, 24, <u>25</u>, 26)
Socio-Economic Class (1, <u>3</u>, 19, 22, 23)
Sons (<u>32</u>)
Sports (6)
Standpoint Theory (<u>16</u>, 18, 22, 29)
Stereotypes (<u>3</u>, 5, 6, <u>8</u>, <u>11</u>, <u>13</u>, <u>16</u>, 20, 26, <u>27</u>, <u>32</u>)
Superwoman Myth (22)

T

Teachers' Classroom Communication (*see* Classroom Communication)
Toys (6, 20, <u>32</u>)
Transgender (<u>3</u>, <u>17</u>)
Two-Culture Approach (2, 6, <u>10</u>, <u>17</u>, 18, 30, <u>32</u>, 34)

V

Violence (*see* Abuse)

W

Weight (*see* Body Image and Physical Appearance)
Woman (*see* Femininity, Mothering, and Working Women)
Work (*see* Gendered Roles, Home/Work and Gendered Labor/Work)
Working Women (1, 2, 5, 9, <u>10</u>, <u>13</u>, <u>17</u>, <u>21</u>, 22, 23, 24, <u>25</u>, 26, <u>27</u>, 33)
Workplace (*see* Organizations)
Work-Life
    "Balance" (<u>13</u>, 19, <u>21</u>, 22, 24, 26)
    Policy (<u>21</u>, 22)

V

Verbal Communication (*see* Language)
Violence (*see* Abuse)

CPSIA information can be obtained
at www.ICGtesting.com
Printed in the USA
FSOW02n0403110315
5653FS